Ecommerce Conversion Checklist

The Ultimate Checklist You Need To Convert All
Visitors To Your Ecommerce Into Satisfied
Customers.Techniques & Strategies Step-by-step For
Beginner to Advanced - More than 300 critical points to
optimize.

Manuel Joseph

Table of Contents

Introduction:

Welcome to the introduction of the book that will guide you through the extraordinary and ever-evolving world of Ecommerce.

These pages are dedicated to you, the entrepreneur or industry professional, who seeks to embrace the challenges and opportunities of today's market to succeed in your growth journey.

In an era where the business landscape is rapidly transforming, it is essential to adapt and leverage the new realities and opportunities to achieve your goals.

The Ecommerce sector has experienced explosive growth in recent years, but not without significant challenges. What worked a few years ago may no longer be suitable today.

With the advent of advanced technologies and changes in consumer preferences, the world of online commerce is undergoing an unprecedented revolution. It is crucial to be aware of what is happening today and anticipate the emerging realities on the horizon.

Our purpose with this book is to guide you through the complexities of the Ecommerce world, providing you with a practical, effective, and up-to-date mental map that will enable you to navigate confidently through the challenges and opportunities you will encounter along your journey. We aim to equip you with the knowledge, tools, and strategies necessary to emerge as a leader in your niche and achieve the success you desire through Ecommerce.

You may be wondering why you should continue reading this book. The answer is simple: because we firmly believe that you can succeed in Ecommerce. Regardless of your level of experience, whether you are a budding entrepreneur or a seasoned professional, what you will learn within these pages will give you the opportunity to stand out from the competition and achieve your personal and professional goals.

You will learn to understand the current challenges of Ecommerce and how to successfully address them. We will explore emerging trends and new technologies that are redefining the way we do business online.

You will be guided through the fundamentals of Ecommerce, with a significant focus on improving the performance and conversions of your online store. You will discover the most effective marketing strategies and how to adapt them to the needs of your target audience. We will provide you with the skills necessary to create an extraordinary shopping experience for your customers, exceeding their expectations and increasing brand loyalty.

Additionally, we will explore the role of artificial intelligence and other emerging technologies in Ecommerce and how you can leverage them to your advantage. We will teach you how to optimize your operations, manage logistics, and protect customer data in compliance with privacy regulations. We will share case studies, practical tips, and industry best practices to help you develop a strategic and effective approach in your Ecommerce growth journey.

We are excited to accompany you on this adventure and share all the knowledge and experience we have gained in the field. We are confident that with commitment and dedication, you can achieve success in your role as an

Ecommerce Manager and reach significant milestones.

Don't miss the opportunity to stand out, anticipate the future, and become the number one in your niche. So, keep reading and immerse yourself in these pages. Take notes, reflect, and put into practice what you learn.

Success in Ecommerce is within your reach, and we are here to guide you along the way.

Enjoy reading and have a fantastic journey in the world of Ecommerce.

Chapter 1: Ecommerce Fundamentals: Everything You Need to Know to Start Strong

Welcome to the world of Ecommerce! In this introductory chapter, we will explore the current landscape and the basic fundamentals you should know to begin your journey towards success in the Ecommerce industry. We will provide you with the essential pillars necessary today to start your path towards building a successful Ecommerce venture.

Whether you're a novice entrepreneur or an experienced professional, what you will learn here will give you a solid foundation on which to build and develop a thriving Ecommerce business, giving it a significant boost in terms of sales.

As mentioned in this first chapter, we will delve into the fundamental principles you should know to embark on your journey towards Ecommerce success. We will cover topics such as the importance of the online realm in the modern commerce landscape, the advantages and disadvantages of Ecommerce, and the key skills required to thrive.

Although Ecommerce has become a pillar of the global market, it is crucial to understand its foundations in order to build a strong base for your business. Let's take a closer look at some of the key concepts.

1.1 The Importance of Ecommerce in the Modern Commerce Landscape

Online commerce has played a prominent role in transforming how people purchase products and services. In 2023, the number of online shoppers continues to steadily rise, driven by the proliferation of mobile devices and increased consumer trust in online purchasing. This trend presents unprecedented opportunities for entrepreneurs and Ecommerce professionals.

Before diving into the details, it's essential to understand the context in which Ecommerce stands in 2023. The industry is experiencing continuous growth, with an increasing number of individuals preferring to shop online rather than at traditional brick-and-mortar stores. The advent of mobile technologies, social media, and artificial intelligence has revolutionized how people shop and interact with various brands.

1.2 Advantages and Disadvantages of Ecommerce

Ecommerce offers numerous advantages compared to traditional commerce. Consumers can conveniently make purchases from the comfort of their homes, compare products and prices with a few clicks, and access a wide range of offerings. On the other hand, there are also disadvantages, such as the lack of tactile shopping experience and the need to ensure the security of online transactions and shipping. Understanding these aspects will help you maximize the benefits and mitigate the challenges.

We have a range of advantages and opportunities for both entrepreneurs and consumers. For entrepreneurs, Ecommerce enables reaching a global audience, overcoming geographical barriers, and expanding their target market. Additionally, opening an online store requires lower initial investment compared to a physical retail location, offering greater flexibility and immediate or near-immediate growth potential.

For consumers, Ecommerce provides convenience, ease of product research, comparison of products and prices, and the ability to access a wide range of products from anywhere in the world that they may not have had access to otherwise. Furthermore, many Ecommerce platforms offer fast and reliable delivery services, making the online shopping experience even more convenient.

1.3 Key Skills for Ecommerce Success

Today, more than ever, Ecommerce requires a range of skills to achieve significant results. Some of the most important skills include website management, understanding digital marketing, knowledge of data analytics tools, and mastery of online selling strategies. Throughout the book, we will delve into each of these skills in detail, providing practical advice and effective tips to steer you towards success.

Before diving into this exciting world, it's crucial to understand these foundations. Familiarizing yourself with the importance of Ecommerce, its advantages and disadvantages, and the key skills required will help you develop a solid foundation for success in your niche.

In the next chapter, we will explore how to create an extraordinary shopping experience to win over customers. We will discuss the importance of website design, usability, and optimization to provide a seamless experience for visitors.

Remember, success in Ecommerce requires a combination of knowledge, strategy, and action. Prepare to further delve into these concepts, implementing best practices and adapting them to your business.

Keep reading to discover how to build a successful website for your Ecommerce business in the next chapter!

Now, let's proceed with Chapter 2 of your book, focused on the importance of creating an extraordinary shopping experience to win over customers.

Let's now explore the keys to success in Ecommerce.

If you want to stand out from the crowd and truly succeed in Ecommerce today, there are some fundamental "rules" to keep in mind or what I like to call "secret keys."

Secret Key #1: You must know your target audience

I know you've heard this phrase before, but believe me, understanding your target audience thoroughly is essential to develop an effective marketing strategy and offer dedicated products and services that meet their needs. Conduct thorough market research, analyze your customer data, and use analytics tools to gain valuable insights into your audience's behavior and preferences.

Secret Key #2: Create a flawless user experience

The user experience on your website is crucial to facilitate users and capture their attention towards your products. Ensure that your site is well-designed, intuitive, easy to navigate, and optimized for mobile devices. Provide secure payment options and simplify the checkout process to minimize cart abandonment. But we'll discuss this in more detail later on.

Secret Key #3: Invest in digital marketing

Given the increasing competition and rising advertising costs, it's important to develop a well-thought-out digital marketing strategy. Utilize a combination of marketing strategies such as pay-per-click (PPC) advertising, content marketing, social media marketing, and email marketing campaigns. Tailor your strategies to the needs of your audience and constantly monitor the results to make any necessary improvements.

Secret Key #4: Provide high-quality customer service

Excellent customer service is one of the best ways to differentiate yourself from the competition and build loyalty towards your brand. Respond promptly to customer inquiries and complaints, offer support through online chat, email, or phone, and always strive to exceed your customers' expectations.

1.4 The Challenges of Ecommerce in 2023

In addition to the current issues related to visitor conversion and increasing advertising costs, there are other challenges that Ecommerce businesses must face today. These include managing logistics and delivery, adapting to new emerging technologies like artificial intelligence and automation, and ensuring the protection of customers' personal data in compliance with privacy regulations.

Addressing these challenges requires strategic planning and ongoing attention to market evolution. Staying updated on the latest trends and adopting innovative solutions will help you maintain a competitive advantage in your industry and stay one step ahead of your competitors.

1.5 The Rapid Evolution of the Technological World and Its Impact on Ecommerce

We live in an era where the world is changing at a rapid pace, driven by technological acceleration. It is crucial to adapt as quickly as possible to new innovations to remain competitive and prepare for the advancements that technology presents. One sector experiencing significant impact is Ecommerce, and one of the technologies redefining how we do business is artificial intelligence (AI).

1.5.1 Artificial Intelligence: Transforming Ecommerce

Artificial intelligence, or AI, is a discipline within computer science that focuses on creating systems that simulate human intelligence. In recent years, AI has made significant advancements due to increased computing power, progress in algorithms, and the availability of large amounts of data.

In the realm of Ecommerce, AI is revolutionizing multiple aspects of the online selling process. One of its most evident applications is in the use of chatbots, which utilize AI to interactively communicate with customers, provide support, and answer their questions. Chatbots can be integrated into Ecommerce websites or messaging apps, allowing customers to receive immediate and personalized assistance.

But AI goes beyond just chatbots. It has the ability to analyze vast amounts of data to identify patterns and trends, helping entrepreneurs make informed decisions regarding marketing strategies, warehouse operations, inventory management, and more. AI can also be used to enhance the shopping experience by personalizing offers and recommendations based on individual customer behavior and preferences.

1.5.2 The Importance of Adopting AI in Ecommerce

The adoption of AI in Ecommerce has become a necessity to remain competitive and fully harness the opportunities offered by technology. Companies that have taken early steps to integrate AI into their processes have gained a significant advantage over others. This is because AI enables the automation of repetitive and routine tasks, improves operational efficiency, and delivers personalized experiences to customers.

AI can analyze customer data to identify their purchasing preferences, create targeted market segments, and develop focused marketing strategies. It can also optimize inventory management by predicting future demand and reducing waste. Additionally, AI can detect and prevent fraud and suspicious activities, enhancing the security of online transactions.

It is important to emphasize that AI will not completely replace human work but rather complement it. Human skills, such as creativity, empathy, and complex problem-solving, remain essential in the context of Ecommerce. AI can support individuals in making better decisions, optimizing operations, and providing more efficient and effective customer service.

1.6 Preparing for the Future of Ecommerce

To prepare for the future of Ecommerce, it is essential to strategically adopt AI and other emerging technologies. Staying updated on the latest trends and technological solutions available for Ecommerce is crucial. Collaborating with experienced AI professionals and forming partnerships with specialized companies can help effectively integrate AI into your business.

Furthermore, it is important to invest in training and foster an innovation-oriented company culture. Educating yourself and your team about the potential of AI and the best practices in utilizing this technology will give you a competitive edge in the Ecommerce industry.

Be open to continuous learning and embrace change as an opportunity for growth and development.

1.7 The Bad News and the Good News

There's some bad news we need to address right away: if you don't take action now and promptly adapt to the current market, you may struggle to survive in the world of Ecommerce.

The reality is that conversion rates are declining, and advertising costs are constantly increasing. Competition has become increasingly aggressive, and if you don't take the right measures, you could fall behind and see your Ecommerce business fail.

Let's talk about declining conversion rates for a moment.

One of the warning signs in the Ecommerce industry is the decrease in conversion rates. Despite the increase in online traffic and sales opportunities, converting visitors into paying customers is becoming increasingly challenging. This can be attributed to various factors, including rising customer expectations, fierce competition, and an ever-expanding array of online alternatives.

Customers have a wide range of choices, and if your Ecommerce business doesn't offer an extraordinary and unique experience, you're likely to lose potential sales.

As for traffic, there's an increase in advertising costs to consider.

Another challenge Ecommerce entrepreneurs must face today revolves around the steadily rising costs of advertising. The growing competition in the industry has led to higher expenses for acquiring new customers through online advertising campaigns.

Platforms like Google Ads, Facebook Ads, Instagram Ads, TikTok Ads, and many others require a progressively significant budget to gain visibility and reach your target audience. This means that if you don't optimize your advertising campaigns and maximize your return on investment, you could end up spending a considerable amount of money without achieving significant results.

Action is needed now!

Faced with these challenges, it is crucial to take action now and take the necessary steps to adapt to today's market. Delaying or ignoring these warning signs could jeopardize the survival of your Ecommerce business.

However, you shouldn't let yourself be overwhelmed by the situation. On the contrary, you should see these challenges as opportunities to differentiate yourself from the competition and grow.

The good news is: Success is still possible!

The good news is that success in Ecommerce is still possible. If you take proactive action and adopt the right strategies, you can overcome these challenges and achieve exceptional results. There are many opportunities in the current market, and those who understand customer needs, offer an outstanding shopping experience, and develop effective marketing strategies can emerge as leaders in their industry in no time.

This book is here to provide you with all the information, strategies, and tools you need to succeed in Ecommerce today. You will learn how to improve the performance and conversions of your Ecommerce business, how to create an extraordinary shopping experience, how to leverage new technologies like artificial intelligence, and how to develop an effective marketing strategy. We will give you the skills necessary to stand out in your niche and outperform the competition.

So, don't wait any longer. Take control of your future in the Ecommerce industry and start taking action right now. Choose to be one of the few who understands the importance of adapting to the current market and take the necessary steps to succeed.

Keep reading this book, and you will discover how to turn challenges into opportunities, achieve remarkable results, and become the leader in your niche in the world of Ecommerce.

1.8 Need for a New Approach

In the industry, it has become evident that a new approach is needed to achieve success. Traditional online selling strategies may no longer be sufficient to stand out from the competition and attract customers.

The Ecommerce landscape has become increasingly competitive and dynamic, calling for a radical change in our strategies and how we tackle challenges.

The Solution: The Importance of Innovation and Strategy

The solution to these challenges lies in innovation and strategy. To succeed in today's Ecommerce market, it is crucial to adopt new solutions and approaches that cater to customer needs and leverage available technologies. It is necessary to go beyond conventions and develop strategies that provide an extraordinary shopping experience, exceed customer expectations, and differentiate from the competition.

So, how do you win in the Ecommerce industry?

In the Ecommerce industry, the winners are those who understand customer needs and effectively meet them in a simple and fast manner. Successful companies invest in creating an exceptional shopping experience, offering quality products, and providing impeccable customer service.

Those who can personalize the shopping experience based on individual customer preferences and anticipate their needs will be able to differentiate themselves from the competition and build a loyal following.

Furthermore, those who make the most of new technologies like artificial intelligence and automation will have a significant advantage over time. AI can help identify market trends, personalize offers, and optimize operations, enabling companies to achieve levels of efficiency and effectiveness never seen before. Those who invest in innovation and fully leverage the potential of technology will be able to adapt quickly to market changes and seize new opportunities.

Who loses in the Ecommerce industry?

On the other hand, those who lose in the Ecommerce industry are those who fail to adapt to change and continue following outdated business models. Those who are unable to offer an extraordinary shopping experience, differentiate themselves from the competition, and meet customer needs will struggle to attract and retain customers. Those who do not invest in innovation and technology, clinging to outdated processes, risk falling behind and being overtaken by more agile and cutting-edge competitors.

Furthermore, those who are unwilling to adapt to new data privacy regulations and customer security requirements risk losing consumer trust and damaging their reputation. Transparency and customer data protection have become fundamental priorities, and those who do not comply with these demands may face negative consequences.

The Importance of Being Ready for Change

In conclusion, to succeed in Ecommerce, it is crucial to adopt a new approach based on innovation and strategy, leveraging the available technologies. Those who can offer an extraordinary shopping experience, make the most of new opportunities, and quickly adapt to market changes will emerge as leaders in the industry.

On the other hand, those who fail to keep up with the pace of change and adapt to the new dynamics of the market may lose their positions and see their Ecommerce struggle to survive.

So, don't wait. Be prepared to embrace change, innovate, and create an extraordinary shopping experience for your customers. This book will guide you through all the information, strategies, and tools you need to succeed in the world of Ecommerce and achieve excellent results.

Keep reading and get ready to seize all the opportunities that the future of Ecommerce has to offer.

Now, let's continue with Chapter 2, focused on the importance of creating an extraordinary shopping experience to win the hearts of your customers.

Chapter 2: Guide to Niche Research: Finding and Conquering Your Ideal Audience

Welcome to this new chapter of the book! In this chapter, we will explore the importance of niche research in the world of Ecommerce. Finding and conquering your ideal audience is crucial for the success of your online store. You will learn how to identify a profitable market niche, understand the needs of your potential customers, and develop a targeted strategy to effectively reach them.

2.1 The Importance of Niche Research

In the vast landscape of Ecommerce, niche research is essential to stand out from the competition and reach a specific audience rather than a generic one. A market niche is a specific segment of customers with well-defined needs, interests, or characteristics. Focusing on a niche allows you to specialize and offer products and services that precisely meet the needs of that audience, creating a significant competitive advantage.

2.2 Identifying a Profitable Niche

The first step in niche research is to identify a profitable niche. To do this, you need to conduct thorough market research. Analyze consumption trends, identify unmet market needs, and evaluate the competition. Look for market segments that are not saturated and present growth opportunities. Also, consider if you already have an existing Ecommerce store or if you have one or more products to sell, they should have a well-defined target market. Otherwise, look into your interests and personal experiences to find something that could help you specialize in a specific industry.

2.3 Understanding Your Ideal Audience

Once you have identified a market niche, it is crucial to understand your ideal audience. Conduct in-depth market research to understand the problems, needs, desires, challenges, and purchasing behaviors of potential customers within your niche. Utilize data analytics tools, surveys, or interviews to gather valuable information. This deep knowledge will allow you to personalize the shopping experience, create relevant content, and develop targeted marketing strategies.

2.4 Developing a Targeted Strategy

Once you understand your ideal audience, it is time to develop a targeted strategy to reach them. Define your unique selling proposition (USP) in the market and identify the strengths that set you apart from the competition. Create a specific value proposition for your audience that addresses their needs and provides effective solutions. Choose the most suitable marketing channels to reach your audience, such as social media, content marketing, or PPC advertising. Customize your messages to effectively communicate with your audience and create an emotional connection with them.

2.5 Monitoring and Adapting

Niche research is a dynamic process that requires constant monitoring and adaptation to the changing market needs. Carefully monitor market trends, customer preferences, and your competitors' strategies. Utilize analytics tools to measure the effectiveness of your marketing strategies and make any necessary changes or optimizations. Stay alert to emerging opportunities and be ready to innovate and adapt accordingly.

2.6 The Key to Success in Niche Research

The key to success in niche research lies in your ability to understand your ideal audience and offer an extraordinary shopping experience. Focus on creating a unique brand, personalizing your offerings, and developing authentic relationships with your customers. Be consistent in delivering value, addressing their needs, and surpassing their expectations. The secret is to create an unforgettable experience that stands out from the crowd.

Chapter 3: Creating an Extraordinary Shopping Experience: The Key to Winning Customers' Hearts

Welcome to the second chapter of the book, where we will explore the importance of creating an extraordinary shopping experience to win the hearts of your customers. As an entrepreneur or Ecommerce professional, understanding the significance of an engaging purchasing experience will give you a tremendous competitive advantage in today's market.

A good shopping experience is essential for attracting and retaining customers, differentiating yourself from the competition, and increasing conversions. You will discover the best practices for offering a unique and memorable experience to your customers, taking into account all aspects of the online purchasing process.

3.1 The crucial role of Ecommerce design

The design of your website is the starting point for creating a memorable shopping experience. Leading Ecommerce platforms like "Amazon," "Zalando," and other industry giants emphasize the importance of intuitive, clean, and visually appealing design to capture visitors' attention and guide them through the purchasing process in the simplest way possible.

Use eye-catching graphics, colors consistent with your brand, and a simple and fast navigation structure to create a visually pleasing and user-friendly environment. Remember that today's online shoppers are not just looking for products or services; they desire a pleasant, simple, and rewarding experience during their purchasing journey.

An extraordinary shopping experience can set you apart from the competition, generate positive reviews, and increase customer loyalty. We will discuss all these aspects in more detail very soon.

3.2 USP (Unique Selling Proposition)

The USP, or Unique Selling Proposition, is what sets your Ecommerce apart from the competition and allows you to effectively communicate the unique value you offer to your customers. Finding your USP accurately and convincingly is essential for standing out in the market and capturing the attention of potential customers. Here are some steps you can follow to identify your USP in the best possible way:

1. Analyze the competition: Study your main competitors carefully to understand how they position themselves and what advantages they offer. Identify their key features and strengths. This analysis will help you identify opportunities to differentiate yourself and find an area where you can excel.

2. Know your target audience: Understanding your audience is crucial for developing a relevant USP. Conduct in-depth market research to identify the needs, desires, and concerns of your potential customers. Try to understand what they are looking for and identify the factors that may influence their purchasing decisions.

3. Identify your unique strengths: Evaluate what makes your Ecommerce unique and

special. It could be a wide selection of products, fast and reliable shipping, exceptional customer service, a favorable return policy, or a competitive pricing range. Identify what sets you apart from your competitors and can provide added value to your customers.

4. Emphasize customer benefits: Focus on the benefits that your customers will gain by choosing your Ecommerce. Consider what makes their experience with you better than other competitors. It could be a seamless shopping experience, product customization, access to educational content, or offering high-quality products. Highlight these benefits in your USP to show customers why they should choose you.

5. Be clear and concise: Your USP should be communicated in a clear and concise manner. Avoid complex or ambiguous language. Choose words and phrases that capture attention and immediately communicate your unique value. Try to condense your USP into a statement of one

or two short paragraphs that can be easily understood by your potential customers.

6. Test and refine: Once you have identified your USP, test and refine it based on customer feedback and the results you achieve. Monitor the effectiveness of your USP closely through metrics such as conversion rate, customer feedback, and differentiation from the competition. If necessary, make changes and improvements to ensure that your USP is authentic, compelling, and aligned with the evolving market.

Remember that your USP is not static but can evolve over time. Always maintain an open mindset and adapt your USP according to the needs of your customers and market opportunities. Once identified and effectively communicated, your USP can become one of the pillars of your Ecommerce success.

3.3 Usability and Ease of Navigation

The usability of your website is essential to provide a seamless shopping experience. Many world-renowned Ecommerce platforms emphasize the importance of well-organized information architecture, efficient search functionality, and simplified checkout processes. Ensure that visitors can easily find what they are looking for, access product information clearly and intuitively, and complete the purchase in a few simple steps. Minimize distractions and friction that may discourage customers from completing the purchase.

Furthermore, optimize your site for mobile devices. More and more people are shopping online through smartphones or tablets, so it is crucial that your site is mobile-friendly and offers a consistent and enjoyable experience across all platforms. Always consider the mobile/desktop ratio as a 90/10 ratio.

3.4 Personalization and Emotional Connection

Creating a personalized shopping experience and establishing an emotional connection with your customers are crucial aspects of Ecommerce success. I want to emphasize the importance of using customer data and information to provide personalized recommendations, targeted marketing messages, and exceptional customer service. Invest in understanding your customers by gathering feedback, analyzing data, and adapting your marketing strategies to their specific needs.

Utilize the data you have collected on your customers to offer personalized offers and suggestions. You can use AI-based recommendation algorithms to suggest related or complementary products to what the customer is viewing or purchasing. Additionally, you can send personalized emails that offer promotions or special offers based on their interests and past purchasing behavior.

3.5 Images and Detailed Product Descriptions

Images and product descriptions are essential for providing information to potential buyers and generating interest in your products. Use high-quality images that showcase the product from various angles and provide an accurate representation of what the customer is purchasing. A useful trick is to contextualize the photo in its use. Add detailed descriptions that include technical specifications, dimensions, materials, and any other relevant information. Additionally, consider including customer reviews directly below the product description to increase trust in the product.

3.6 Mobile Optimization

In 2023, the number of purchases made from mobile devices continues to grow significantly. It is crucial to optimize your website and the purchasing process for mobile devices to provide a seamless experience across all devices. "Mobile Commerce Mastery" by Chris Johnson provides advice on creating responsive design, improving page loading times, and streamlining the checkout process for visitors using smartphones and tablets.

3.7 Customer Assistance and Support

Another crucial component of an extraordinary shopping experience is customer assistance and support. Ensure that you provide customers with various options to contact customer service, such as live chat, email, or phone. Respond promptly to customer questions and complaints, and strive to exceed their expectations by providing solutions and assistance. I will never stop emphasizing this: Exceed their expectations. Surprise them! Do something extra that they don't expect. Send them an exclusive complimentary product, offer them a 50% discount on their next order, entice them to come back to you in any way possible. Additionally, consider implementing a Frequently Asked Questions (FAQ) section to address common customer questions and concerns, improving the efficiency of customer service.

3.8 Facilitating the Checkout Process

The checkout process is a critical stage in the purchase journey and should be as simple and smooth as possible. Minimize the number of mandatory fields in the payment form and offer various payment options such as credit cards, PayPal, or other popular electronic payment solutions. Ensure that the checkout process is secure and protected by data encryption technologies to reassure customers about the safety of their personal information. But we'll discuss this further ahead.

3.9 Efficient Delivery and Returns

Another crucial component of an extraordinary shopping experience involves product delivery and the returns process. Offer different shipping options such as standard shipping, express shipping, or in-store pickup to cater to customers' diverse needs. Clearly communicate delivery times and provide a tracking number to allow customers to monitor the status of their shipment. Additionally, streamline the returns process and provide efficient customer service in handling any post-sale issues or complaints.

3.10 Social Proof and Customer Reviews

The opinions of others play a decisive role in online purchasing decisions. Amazon, for instance, has been a pioneer in online reviews, highlighting the importance of customer reviews and social proof in building trust and encouraging sales. Implement tools to gather authentic customer reviews, showcase positive testimonials, and provide a platform for users to share their experiences. Also, leverage social media to promote positive reviews and engage customers in sharing their experiences.

3.11 Measuring and Optimizing the Purchase Experience

Lastly, it is crucial to continuously measure and optimize the purchase experience to ensure ongoing improvement. Use analytics tools to monitor customer behavior on your site, such as pages visited, time spent, and conversion rates. Analyze the data to identify any weaknesses or areas for improvement and take necessary measures to optimize the purchase experience.

In this chapter, we have explored the importance of creating an extraordinary shopping experience to win customers in today's competitive market. We have discussed website design, usability, personalization, mobile optimization, social proof, and much more. Use this information to enhance the shopping experience on your Ecommerce site and leave a lasting positive impression on your customers.

In the next chapter, we will delve into winning marketing strategies to promote your Ecommerce business. You will discover how to leverage best practices in digital marketing to increase the visibility of your website, generate qualified traffic, and maximize sales.

Keep reading to uncover how to achieve exceptional results through conversion design and cutting-edge marketing strategies! Let's proceed with the development of Chapter 3, now focusing on winning marketing strategies to promote your Ecommerce business. I will continue to take into account the instructions you have provided earlier. Here is the third chapter of your book.

Chapter 4: Winning Marketing Strategies to Promote Your Ecommerce Business

Welcome to the third chapter of the book, dedicated to winning marketing strategies to promote your Ecommerce business in the best possible way. Understanding and utilizing the best practices in digital marketing will allow you to increase the visibility of your website, generate qualified traffic, and maximize sales.

4.1 Search Engine Optimization (SEO)

Search Engine Optimization (SEO) is a fundamental strategy for improving the visibility of your Ecommerce business and positioning yourself as relevant and authoritative in the eyes of customers and search engines.

We want to highlight the importance of accurate keyword research, creating high-quality content, optimizing pages and website structure to rank well in search engines.

Use relevant keywords in your content, optimize title and description tags, create SEO-friendly URLs, and pay attention to site loading speed to ensure a strong and well-positioned online presence.

Search Engine Optimization (SEO) is a crucial practice for attracting high-quality organic traffic. Here are some key points to consider for effectively leveraging this technique in your Ecommerce business:

1. Keyword research: Conduct thorough research on relevant keywords for your industry and products. Identify keywords with significant search volume and reasonable competition. Use keyword research tools like Google Keyword Planner, SEMrush, or Moz Keyword Explorer to find the most relevant keywords for your business.

2. Content optimization: Strategically use keywords within your content, but in a natural and organic manner. Include keywords in the page title, headers (H1, H2, etc.), meta descriptions, image tags, and internal links. Ensure that your content

is high-quality, relevant to users, and addresses the questions and needs of your potential customers.

3. Website structure: Create a well-organized and intuitive website structure. Use a consistent URL hierarchy where important pages are easily accessible with a few clicks from the homepage. Ensure that search engines can easily access and index all pages of your site through clear information architecture.

4. Website speed: Website loading speed is an important factor for SEO optimization. Ensure that your site is fast and responsive, both on desktop and mobile devices. Reduce image file sizes, minimize HTML, JavaScript, and CSS code, and use a reliable hosting solution to ensure optimal performance.

5. Quality backlinks: Backlinks, which are links pointing to your site from other web pages, are a signal of trust and authority for search engines. Seek to obtain quality backlinks from authoritative sources in your industry. You can do this by creating compelling content that people will want

to share and link to, participating in guest posting on relevant blogs, or actively engaging on social media.

6. User experience: Provide an excellent user experience on your website. Ensure that your site is easy to navigate, with intuitive information architecture and appealing design. Minimize page loading times, ensuring that your site is accessible and usable on mobile devices. Offer valuable content and simple navigation to make the user experience enjoyable and satisfying.

7. Monitoring and analysis: Use web analytics tools like Google Analytics to monitor the performance of your website. Analyze key metrics such as organic traffic, conversion rate, and user behavior. Identify strengths and areas for improvement, and make necessary optimizations based on the data collected.

Remember that SEO optimization is an ongoing process and takes time to achieve significant results. Maintain a consistent SEO strategy over time and stay updated on the latest trends and best practices in the industry. By properly implementing SEO optimization in your

Ecommerce business, you can increase the visibility of your website, attract quality traffic, and improve your conversions.

4.2 Online Advertising and Pay-Per-Click (PPC)

Online advertising, including pay-per-click (PPC) advertising, can be an effective way to generate qualified traffic to your Ecommerce business. Bestsellers like "Advertising for Ecommerce Success" by Sarah Johnson emphasize the importance of strategic ad planning, accurate audience segmentation, and careful selection of advertising platforms. Explore tools such as Google Ads, Facebook Ads, and Instagram Ads to reach your target audience by creating engaging ads and offering incentives to attract potential customers.

Pay-per-click (PPC) is a powerful tool for driving qualified traffic to your Ecommerce business. Here are some key points to consider for making the most of this form of advertising:

Identifying advertising channels: First and foremost, identify the most appropriate online advertising channels to reach your target audience. Common channels include Google Ads (formerly Google AdWords), Facebook Ads, Instagram Ads, Twitter Ads, LinkedIn Ads, TikTok Ads, and others. Evaluate the demographic characteristics, interests, and user behavior on each platform to determine which one is best for promoting your products.

Setting advertising objectives: Before launching an advertising campaign, establish specific objectives you wish to achieve. You may want to increase sales, generate leads, enhance brand awareness, or promote a new product. Clearly defining your goals will help structure your campaign and measure the results.

Keyword research: If you're using Google Ads, keyword research is crucial. Identify relevant keywords that users might type in their search queries to find products or services like yours. Use tools like Google Keyword Planner to identify keywords with good search volume and reasonable competition. Organize your keywords into thematic groups and create targeted ads for each group.

Creating effective ads: Ensure that your ads are catchy, relevant, and compelling to your target audience. Use attention-grabbing headlines, clear and enticing descriptions, and utilize ad extensions to provide additional information or call-to-action (CTA). Incorporate engaging images or videos to capture users' attention.

Demographic and geographic targeting: Utilize targeting options available on different advertising channels to reach your specific audience. You can set demographic parameters such as age, gender, occupation, and interests to reach people who are more likely to be interested in your products. You can also set geographic targeting to focus on specific geographical areas where you want to promote your Ecommerce business.

Monitoring and optimization: Continuously monitor the performance of your advertising campaigns and make necessary optimizations. Analyze key metrics such as click-through rate (CTR), cost per click (CPC), conversion rate, and return on investment (ROI). Use the collected data to optimize your campaigns, such as adjusting bids, modifying keywords, creating new ads, or adding extensions.

Budget and testing: Establish an appropriate budget for your advertising campaigns and distribute it strategically. Test different strategies, such as different keywords, ad texts, or images, to identify what works best for your audience. A/B testing is an effective way to compare two different versions of an ad and determine which one generates better results.

Remember that online advertising and PPC require careful and consistent management. Regularly monitor your campaigns, make changes and optimizations, and leverage the collected data to improve your ad performance. With a strategic and well-planned approach, online advertising can be an effective means to drive qualified traffic to your Ecommerce business and increase sales.

4.3 Social Media Marketing

Social media provides a tremendous opportunity to promote your Ecommerce business and engage directly with your audience. Bestsellers like "Social Media Strategies for Ecommerce" by David Wilson highlight the importance of consistent and engaging social media presence. Identify the social media platforms that are most suitable for your target customers and use them to share valuable content, engage your audience, manage customer service, and promote special offers. Leverage influencers and collaborations to increase your brand visibility as well.

Social media offers a unique opportunity to connect with your audience, build brand awareness, and promote your products. You will learn the fundamental strategies to make the most of social media marketing and achieve effective results for your business.

Social media marketing has become an essential element in the marketing strategy of any online business. Social media platforms provide a large user base and enable businesses to reach their target audience directly and effectively. In addition to simply promoting products, social media offers the opportunity to build an authentic relationship with your customers, gather feedback, and provide excellent customer service.

The first phase of social media marketing is identifying which social platforms are most relevant to your target audience and industry. Facebook, Instagram, Twitter, LinkedIn,

Pinterest, and YouTube are just some of the available options. Evaluate the demographic characteristics, interests, and behaviors of your potential customers to determine which platforms are most suitable for promoting your products and engaging with your audience.

An effective content strategy is crucial for the success of social media marketing. Create an editorial plan that includes the types of content you want to share, the timing of posts, and ways to engage your audience. Use a combination of textual, visual, and video content to maintain your audience's interest. Provide valuable content such as tips, tutorials, success stories, or behind-the-scenes glimpses of your Ecommerce business.

Social media provides a unique opportunity to interact directly with your audience. Respond to comments, private messages, and reviews promptly and professionally. Use polling or question features in stories to engage your audience and gather direct feedback. Organize contests or promotions to stimulate interaction and encourage users to share your brand with their contacts.

Social media platforms also offer advertising options to increase your brand visibility and reach a wider audience. Use targeting tools to identify your ideal audience and display relevant ads to people with specific interests, demographics, or behaviors. Choose from advertising formats such as paid ads, sponsored stories, carousel ads, or video ads to creatively and effectively promote your products.

Remember that social media marketing requires ongoing effort and monitoring. Regularly analyze your performance, adjust your strategies, and leverage analytics to optimize your social media presence. With a well-executed and strategic approach, social media marketing can be a powerful tool to drive brand awareness, engage your audience, and ultimately increase sales for your Ecommerce business.

Monitor the performance of your social media marketing activities regularly using the analytics tools available on each platform. Analyze key metrics such as engagement, follower count, link clicks, and conversion rate. Use the collected data to evaluate the effectiveness of your strategy, identify top-performing content or campaigns, and make necessary optimizations to improve results.

Lastly, to achieve long-lasting results with social media marketing, it is crucial to maintain a consistent and cohesive presence. Regularly publish high-quality content, respond to questions and interactions from your followers, and keep your brand top of mind for potential customers. Build an authentic relationship with your audience and provide consistent value to create loyalty and trust.

4.4 Content Marketing

I want to emphasize the importance of creating quality content such as blogs, buying guides, video tutorials, and webinars to educate your audience and position yourself as an expert in your industry. Utilize SEO strategies to optimize your content and promote it through social channels, newsletters, and collaborations with other influencers or industry websites.

Content marketing provides an opportunity to actively engage your audience. Respond to comments and questions from your readers, encourage them to share their experiences and provide feedback. Foster an open and authentic dialogue with your audience to create a stronger connection and build lasting relationships.

4.5 Email Marketing and Automation

Email marketing remains one of the most powerful channels for engaging customers and increasing sales. Here, we emphasize the importance of creating qualified contact lists, sending personalized and relevant emails, and utilizing segmentation and automation to deliver targeted content and offers. Provide value to your subscribers through informative newsletters, exclusive discounts, tips, and industry insights.

In this chapter, we have explored various winning marketing strategies to promote your e-commerce business. We have covered search engine optimization (SEO), online advertising, social media marketing, content marketing, and email marketing.

Utilize these strategies strategically and tailor your actions to the needs of your target audience.

In the next chapter, we will explore best practices to maximize conversions on your e-commerce platform. You will learn how to optimize the purchasing process, manage abandoned carts, and utilize up-selling and cross-selling strategies to increase the average order value.

Keep reading to discover how to improve your conversions and achieve exceptional results!

Let's proceed with the development of Chapter 5 of your e-commerce book, focused on the best practices to maximize conversions. I will continue to take into account the instructions you have provided earlier. Here is the fourth chapter of your book.

Chapter 5: Maximizing Conversions

Welcome to the fourth chapter of the book, dedicated to the best practices for maximizing conversions on your e-commerce platform. Conversion is the heart of your online business success, so it is essential to implement effective strategies to increase the number of visits that result in sales.

5.1 Optimization of the purchasing process

Optimizing the purchasing process is crucial to simplify the customer experience and reduce friction during the conversion process. Here, we highlight the importance of intuitive navigation, a smooth checkout process, and a hassle-free user experience. Minimize the steps required to complete a purchase, simplify registration and checkout access, and provide clear instructions at each step of the funnel. We will delve into this further shortly.

5.2 Abandoned cart management

The abandoned cart is a common challenge in the e-commerce world, but it can also be a great opportunity to recover lost sales. Here, we emphasize the importance of implementing follow-up strategies to engage customers who have added one or more products to their cart but then abandoned it. Use personalized emails with special promotions, offer real-time assistance through chat or chatbots, or consider providing discounts or exclusive offers to persuade undecided customers to return and complete the purchase.

5.3 Up-selling and cross-selling

Up-selling and cross-selling strategies can increase the average order value and improve conversions. Bestsellers like "The Power of Upselling and Cross-selling" by Mark Thompson highlight the importance of offering related or higher-value products to those selected by customers during the purchase process or in the post-purchase phase. Show personalized recommendations on the product page, offer advantageous packages or bundles, and use automation tools to suggest similar or complementary products.

5.4 Customer reviews and testimonials

Customer reviews have a significant impact on the trust of potential buyers. Bestsellers like "The Power of Customer Reviews" by Jessica Adams highlight the importance of collecting and displaying authentic and positive reviews of your products and services. Provide potential buyers with the opportunity to read the experiences of satisfied customers and use reliable review tools to acquire and manage positive feedback.

5.5 A/B testing and continuous optimization

Conversion optimization is an ongoing process. Bestsellers like "Conversion Optimization Mastery" by David Wilson emphasize the importance of conducting A/B tests and experiments to continuously improve the performance of your e-commerce platform. Test different variants of key elements such as call-to-action buttons, product images, descriptions, or prices to identify which elements generate better results. Use analytics tools to monitor key metrics and make data-informed decisions.

In this chapter, we have explored the best practices for maximizing conversions on your e-commerce platform. We have covered the optimization of the purchasing process, abandoned cart management, up-selling and cross-selling strategies, the importance of customer reviews, and continuous optimization through A/B testing.

Now, here is a checklist summarizing the key areas and optimization points you should immediately check on your e-commerce platform to maximize performance and conversions:

1. **User experience:**

   - Intuitive and easy-to-use navigation

   - Optimal page loading speed

   - Engaging and responsive design

   - Simplicity in the purchasing process and checkout

2. **Search engine optimization (SEO):**

   - Research relevant keywords and optimize content accordingly

- Use appropriate meta tags and descriptions

- Create optimized and readable URLs

- Well-organized site structure and proper page indexing

3. Quality content:

- Clear, detailed, and compelling product descriptions

- High-quality and relevant product images

- Informative content such as guides or blogs related to the industry or offered products

4. Offer personalization:

- Collect and utilize customer data for personalized offers

- Targeted promotions and discounts based on purchasing behavior

5. Customer reviews and testimonials:

- Display positive customer reviews and testimonials to build trust

- Use badges or security certifications to reassure customers

6. Social media marketing:

- Active presence on social media platforms relevant to your target audience

- Create engaging and shareable content

- Interact and engage with the audience through comment replies and messages

7. Online advertising and pay-per-click (PPC):

- Utilize targeted and relevant ads on advertising platforms like Google Ads and social media ads

- Continuously monitor and optimize advertising campaigns

8. Email marketing strategy:

- Build a quality contact list

- Send personalized and relevant emails

- Use automation to send targeted messages based on user behavior

9. Data monitoring and analysis:

- Utilize web analytics tools to monitor key metrics such as conversion rate, average order value, and user journey

- Analyze data to identify strengths, weaknesses, and optimization opportunities

10. Testing and continuous optimization:

- Use A/B testing to compare different variations of pages, texts, call-to-action buttons, and offers

- Make optimizations based on test results and continue testing to consistently improve performance

Once you have checked these points and made the necessary modifications and improvements to your e-commerce platform, you will see an immediate increase in conversion rates and give a significant boost to your e-commerce and sales. Remember to adapt these strategies and points to the needs of your specific audience and continuously monitor and optimize for ongoing success.

In the next chapter, we will explore logistics and order management in the world of e-commerce. You will learn how to ensure quality service, manage inventory, and meet customer expectations to create a solid foundation for the long-term success of your e-commerce business.

Keep reading to discover how to effectively manage logistics and provide impeccable service!

Let's proceed with Chapter 6 of the book, which will address logistics and order management in the world of e-commerce.

Chapter 6: Logistics and Order Management in Ecommerce

Welcome to the sixth chapter of the book, dedicated to logistics and order management in the world of e-commerce. Logistics and effective order management are crucial to ensure quality service and meet customer expectations. Let's explore the key aspects of this important phase of e-commerce operations.

6.1 Inventory Management

Inventory management is a crucial aspect of e-commerce. Now we want to emphasize the importance of accurate planning, stock level management, and the use of dedicated systems and software. Make sure to keep track of your products, monitor demand and replenishment, and optimize procurement processes to avoid shortages or overproduction.

6.2 Shipping and Logistics Systems

Choosing an efficient shipping and logistics system is essential to ensure fast delivery times and quality service to customers. Evaluate different shipping options, strive to negotiate competitive rates with couriers, track shipments, and provide accurate tracking information. Select the right logistics partners and implement systems to handle returns and reverse logistics efficiently.

6.3 Customer Service and Post-Sales Support

Excellent customer service and post-sales support are essential to build a base of loyal and satisfied customers. Aim to provide timely responses, resolve issues quickly, and handle customer inquiries with courtesy and empathy. Utilize tools such as real-time chat, email, or phone support services to deliver high-quality customer service that exceeds expectations.

6.4 Return Processes and Refund Policies

Managing returns and refund policies is a crucial aspect of order management in e-commerce. You must have clear and transparent policies, facilitate the return process for customers, and efficiently handle returns. Clearly communicate your return policies and provide flexible options to customers to ensure their satisfaction.

6.5 Process Optimization and Automation

Process optimization and automation are powerful tools to improve efficiency and reduce errors in order management. Identify critical points in your processes, use automation tools to streamline repetitive tasks, and implement efficient workflows. Evaluate processes within your e-commerce operations and look for opportunities to improve and optimize in every area.

In this chapter, we have explored logistics and order management in e-commerce. We have addressed inventory management, shipping and logistics systems, customer service and post-sales support, return processes and refund policies, as well as process optimization and automation.

In the next chapter, we will explore strategies to build a strong online reputation and manage your presence on marketplaces and reviews. You will learn how to influence buyer opinions and maintain a good online reputation.

Keep reading to discover how to manage your online presence and build a solid reputation!

Let's move on to the next chapter of the book, which will focus on managing online presence and building a strong reputation.

Chapter 7: Managing Online Presence and Building Reputation

Welcome to the sixth chapter of the book, dedicated to managing online presence and building a solid reputation for your Ecommerce business. In a constantly evolving digital world, your online presence and the perception customers have of your brand are key elements for the success of your business. Let's explore strategies to manage your online presence and build a strong reputation.

7.1 Brand Consistency and Visual Identity

Brand consistency is crucial in creating a strong and recognizable image for your Ecommerce business. I want to emphasize the importance of defining your brand identity, including the logo, colors, and visual elements, and using them consistently across all communication channels. Ensure that your brand is recognizable and consistent, both on your website and on social media, to create familiarity and build trust with customers.

7.2 Online Reputation Management

Online reputation is crucial for the success of your Ecommerce business. It is important to constantly monitor what is being said about your brand online and respond promptly and effectively to customer reviews and feedback. Handle negative reviews professionally by addressing issues and offering appropriate solutions. Also, leverage positive reviews by sharing them on your channels and using them as a promotional tool.

7.3 Marketplace Presence Management

Marketplaces like Amazon and eBay offer immense visibility and sales opportunities for your Ecommerce business. I want to highlight the importance of strategically managing your presence on marketplaces. Optimize your product pages with captivating images, detailed descriptions, and authentic reviews. Monitor the performance of your listings closely and take advantage of the promotion and advertising options offered by the marketplaces themselves to increase the visibility of your products.

7.4 Social Media Engagement and Community Management

Social media provides a direct channel to engage with your customers and build a loyal community. Now, let's emphasize the importance of engaging your audience on social media by responding to comments, posting interesting content, and participating in conversations. Create an active community, encourage customers to share their experiences, and make your customers feel valued by responding to questions and comments promptly.

7.5 Metric Monitoring and Data Analysis

Monitoring metrics and analyzing data are essential to evaluate the effectiveness of your online presence management strategies. Defining key metrics to monitor, such as website visits, conversions, cart abandonment rates, and customer reviews, is an important step that many overlook. Use analytics tools like Google Analytics to gain valuable insights and make informed decisions to improve your online presence.

In this chapter, we have explored managing online presence and building reputation for your Ecommerce business. We have addressed brand consistency and visual identity, online reputation management, marketplace presence management, social media engagement and community management, as well as metric monitoring and data analysis.

In the next chapter, we will explore emerging trends in Ecommerce and how to adapt to them to remain competitive. You will discover new technologies, changes in consumer behavior, and innovative strategies to drive your Ecommerce business to success in the future.

Let's continue with Chapter 8 of the book, which will explore emerging trends in the industry and innovative strategies to remain competitive.

Chapter 8: The Ecommerce Funnel

Here is a chapter dedicated to the importance of having an effective Conversion Funnel in your Ecommerce:

Many companies consider the Funnel as something external to their Ecommerce site, but they are mistaken. The importance of having an optimized Conversion Funnel in Ecommerce is vital today.

In the world of Ecommerce, the success of online sales depends on the ability to convert visitors into paying customers. But how can this be achieved systematically and predictably? The answer lies in implementing an effective Conversion Funnel.

What is a Conversion Funnel?

A Conversion Funnel represents the path that a visitor takes from the moment they arrive on your Ecommerce site until they complete a desired action, such as purchasing a product. It is a series of targeted and strategically planned steps that guide visitors through the purchasing process and encourage them to take desired actions.

A well-structured Conversion Funnel is essential to maximize your online marketing and sales efforts. That's why it is so important.

Now I'm going to unveil what exactly the Funnel of an Ecommerce is and how to evaluate data at each point of the Funnel.

For the first time, it is necessary to grow your business with proven marketing systems to obtain orders, customers, and contacts with predictable and scientific acquisition.

This is actually what we mean by **"Funnel of an Ecommerce."**

Take a look at this image.

What you see above is the Funnel of an Ecommerce. If you don't know what a Funnel is, don't worry, you can simply imagine it as a sequence of steps that your potential customer needs to follow, whether online or offline, to make a purchase.

In this case, out of 6,546 content views generated by a Facebook advertising campaign, a certain percentage (around 10%), which is 625, added a product to the cart. Subsequently, a good portion of those who added a product to the cart, specifically 372 (over 50%), started the checkout phase by entering their information for the purchase. Finally, approximately 40% or 158 people actually completed the purchase on the website, generating an order.

Conversion rate: 2.4% in this example, calculated as follows:

(number of conversions/unique visitors) x 100

That is: $(158/6,546*100) = 2.4\%$

An excellent conversion rate for these times.

The numbers you see are real! They are not randomly written.

Here are some images that show concrete and tangible results.

Oggi   Questa settimana   Questo mese

giovedì 9 feb

5.401,34€

Fatturato

38   **1,4k**   **2,8%**

Ordini   Visitatori   Conversione

$2k

$1k

12 AM   5 AM   10 AM   3 PM   8 PM

Scopri Di Più

Il mio negozio

Oggi   Questa settimana   Questo mese

domenica 10 apr

$4,920.71

Fatturato

109	3,5k	3,1%
Ordini	Visitatori	Conversione

$600

$300

12 AM   5 AM   10 AM   3 PM   8 PM

Il mio negozio

Oggi   Questa settimana   Questo mese

sabato 9 apr

$6,859.53

Fatturato

114	3,8k	3,0%
Ordini	Visitatori	Conversione

$2k

$1k

12 AM   5 AM   10 AM   3 PM   8 PM

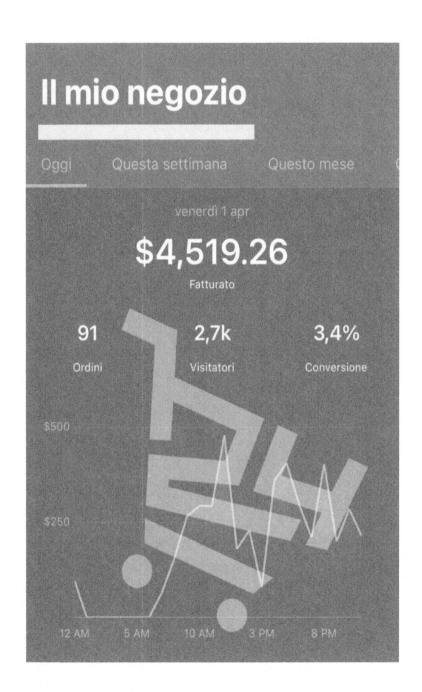

Il mio negozio

Oggi   Questa settimana   Questo mese

venerdì 1 apr

$4,519.26

Fatturato

91	2,7k	3,4%
Ordini	Visitatori	Conversione

$500

$250

12 AM   5 AM   10 AM   3 PM   8 PM

Il mio negozio

Oggi   Questa settimana   Questo mese

martedì 8 mar

4.209,86€

Fatturato

92	1,4k	6,6%
Ordini	Visitatori	Conversione

900€

450€

12 AM   5 AM   10 AM   3 PM   8 PM

Il mio negozio

Oggi Questa settimana Questo mese Qu

venerdì 26 nov

Visitatori	Ordini	Fatturato
3,9k	318	21,6k€

3900/318=12,2%
Capacità di Conversione

1,1k€

-229€

12 AM 5 AM 10 AM 3 PM 8 PM

Aggiornamento effettuato alcuni momenti fa

I MIGLIORI ESECUTORI

Il mio negozio

Oggi   Questa settimana   Questo mese

domenica 10 apr

$4,846.89

Fatturato

107 **3,5k** **3,0%**

Ordini   Visitatori   Conversione

$600

$300

12 AM   5 AM   10 AM   3 PM   8 PM

Oggi Questa settimana Questo mese

lunedì 6 feb

5.260,65€

Fatturato

33	1,7k	1,9%
Ordini	Visitatori	Conversione

2k€

1k€

12 AM   5 AM   10 AM   3 PM   8 PM

Scopri di più

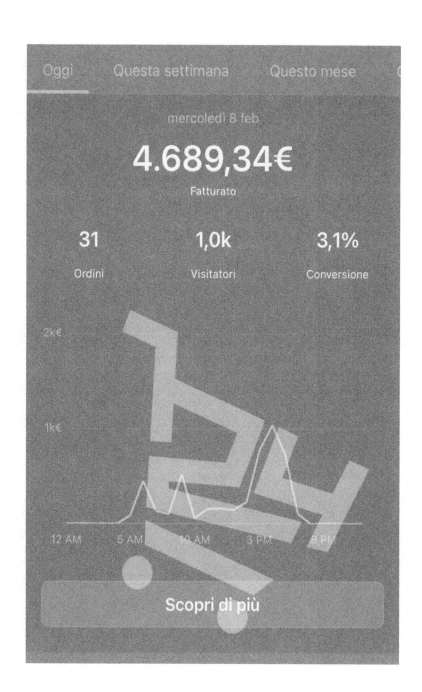

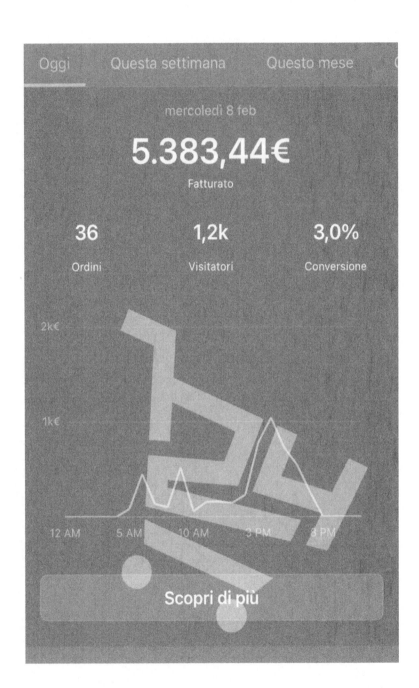

But what are the 5 biggest mistakes made by most Ecommerce businesses? Working as an Ecommerce Manager for the past 7 years, I have learned that most of the mistakes that literally kill conversions in an online store can be counted on one hand.

Primarily, if your store lacks clarity, does not have a strong Unique Value Proposition (UVP), fails to convey needs, desires, trust, and overwhelms visitors with unnecessary details, then it will never reach its full potential in terms of sales, profits, daily orders, and conversions.

Quite the opposite, in fact. After thoroughly examining dozens of online stores, I have noticed that almost ALL Store Managers make the same 5 mistakes that literally kill conversions. Here they are:

Lack of clarity: Their website lacks clarity, credibility, and a strong Unique Value Proposition (UVP), leading to a lack of trust from visitors.

Wrong marketing approach: Their website or marketing system is completely wrong. They immediately focus on selling instead of guiding and educating visitors according to their specific needs.

Complicated checkout process: They make their cart-to-checkout process unnecessarily complex.

Incomplete product pages: Their product pages lack crucial and essential "key" selling elements necessary to convert as many users as possible.

Poor mobile shopping experience: They fail to offer an exceptional and fast mobile shopping experience.

These are the main areas that most Ecommerce businesses overlook and neglect. These are the very areas that are preventing your online business from truly taking off and significantly improving the performance of your store.

Now let's take a brief overview of the emerging trends in the world of Ecommerce.

Chapter 9: Emerging Trends in Ecommerce and Innovative Strategies

Welcome to this new chapter of the book, dedicated to emerging trends in the Ecommerce industry and innovative strategies to remain competitive in today's market. Ecommerce is a constantly evolving sector, and understanding the latest trends will allow you to adapt and capitalize on new growth opportunities. Let's explore some of the most relevant trends and innovative strategies for success in the future of Ecommerce.

9.1 Artificial Intelligence and Automation

Artificial intelligence (AI) and automation are revolutionizing Ecommerce, offering opportunities for personalization, operational optimization, and improved customer experience. I want to emphasize the importance of using AI for data analysis, demand forecasting, customer support through chatbots, and automation of marketing processes. Explore how

AI can enhance your efficiency and customer experience to gain a competitive advantage.

9.2 Voice Commerce

The growth of voice assistants and smart speakers has opened new opportunities for voice commerce, highlighting the importance of optimizing your Ecommerce for voice searches and providing a seamless shopping experience through voice commands. Consider implementing voice search capabilities, integration with voice assistants like Alexa or Google Assistant, and optimizing your product catalog for voice queries.

9.3 Mobile Commerce and Progressive Web Apps

Mobile commerce continues to grow, and Progressive Web Apps (PWAs) are becoming increasingly popular. Here, the importance of having a mobile-optimized shopping experience and offering app-like functionalities through PWAs comes into play. Ensure that your website is responsive and provides a smooth browsing experience on mobile devices. Also, consider the possibility of developing a PWA to offer an app-like experience without requiring the download of a dedicated app.

9.4 Advanced Personalization

Advanced personalization has become a fundamental trend in Ecommerce. In this case, we highlight the importance of offering personalized recommendations and content based on customer data. Utilize AI and machine learning algorithms to analyze customer behavior, their past purchases, and preferences to deliver targeted offers and a personalized shopping experience.

9.5 Sustainability and Social Responsibility

Sustainability and social responsibility are increasingly relevant topics in the world of Ecommerce. Strive to adopt sustainable practices in production, packaging, and product shipping. Consider the use of recyclable materials, offering eco-friendly shipping options, and participating in corporate social responsibility programs to create a positive impact and attract environmentally conscious consumers.

In this chapter, we have explored some of the emerging trends in the Ecommerce industry and innovative strategies to remain competitive. We have covered artificial intelligence and automation, voice commerce, mobile commerce and Progressive Web Apps, advanced personalization, and sustainability.

In the next chapter, we will explore growth and expansion strategies for your Ecommerce. You will discover how to scale your business, reach new markets, and expand your customer base. Keep reading to uncover how to grow your Ecommerce and achieve new milestones!

Let's proceed with the next chapter of the book on Ecommerce, which will explore growth and expansion strategies for your business.

Chapter 10: Growth and Expansion Strategies for Your Ecommerce Business

Welcome to this chapter of the book, dedicated to growth and expansion strategies for your Ecommerce business. Once you have established your Ecommerce, it is crucial to plan and implement effective strategies to reach new milestones and expand your customer base. Let's explore some key strategies for the growth and expansion of your business.

10.1 Scaling your business

Scaling your business means creating a solid structure that allows you to manage an increase in sales volume and customers. Here, strategic planning, process automation, team expansion, and inventory management come into play. Evaluate opportunities to automate repetitive tasks, implement a scalable inventory management system, and consider hiring qualified staff to support the growth of your Ecommerce.

10.2 Geographic expansion

Geographic expansion is an option to reach new markets and expand the reach of your Ecommerce. Conduct market research, adapt your offering to the needs of new markets, and address logistical and legal challenges. Consider expanding your operations to new countries or regions, taking into account cultural, linguistic, and regulatory requirements.

10.3 Collaborations and partnerships

Collaborations and partnerships can be a great strategy to expand your customer base and reach new audiences. Identify partners complementary to your industry and explore collaboration opportunities. Consider creating joint ventures, affiliate programs, or partnerships with influencers or other companies that have a similar audience to yours. These partnerships can help you reach new customers and increase brand visibility.

10.4 Product catalog expansion

Expanding your product catalog can be a strategy to attract new customers and generate additional sales opportunities. Understand the needs of your target customers and identify complementary products or new product categories to offer. Evaluate the opportunity to expand your assortment based on customer demands and market trends to cater to a wider range of needs and desires.

10.5 Customer retention and loyalty program

Retaining existing customers is equally important as attracting new customers. Here, I want to emphasize the importance of developing loyalty programs, offering exclusive discounts, promoting special offers, and providing exceptional customer service. Implement a loyalty program that rewards regular customers, incentivizes customers to return for future purchases, and encourages positive word-of-mouth.

In this chapter, we have explored some key strategies for the growth and expansion of your Ecommerce business. We have covered business scaling, geographic expansion, collaborations and partnerships, product catalog expansion, and customer retention.

In the next chapter, we will provide an overview of best practices for long-term Ecommerce success and some final tips to become the number one in your niche before delving into the Conversion Optimization Checklist. Keep reading to discover the latest best practices and tips for your Ecommerce success!

Let's proceed with the next chapter of the book, which will offer an overview of best practices for long-term Ecommerce success and some final tips to become the number one in your niche.

Chapter 11: Best Practices for Long-Term Ecommerce Success

Welcome to this new chapter of the book, dedicated to best practices for long-term Ecommerce success. At this point, you have gained a solid knowledge and understanding of key strategies and trends in Ecommerce. In this final chapter, we will explore the best practices that will help you solidify your success and become the number one in your niche.

11.1 Focus on the customer experience

Always remember that the customer experience is at the core of a successful business. Putting customers first, providing a seamless shopping experience, responding to customer questions and feedback in a timely and efficient manner, and exceeding their expectations is the best way to do it. Always keep your focus on customer satisfaction and needs, continually seeking to improve and personalize the experience you offer them.

11.2 Monitor key metrics

Monitoring key metrics is essential to assess the success of your business and identify improvement opportunities. Identify and track relevant metrics such as conversions, cart abandonment rate, average order value, and return on investment from marketing campaigns. Utilize analytics tools like Google Analytics to gain valuable insights and make data-driven decisions.

11.3 Maintain a consistent brand image

Consistency in brand image is crucial to create a recognizable identity and build trust with your customers. Strive to maintain a consistent brand image across all communication channels, including your website, social media, email communication, and marketing materials. Ensure that your brand is recognizable and consistently conveys the values and personality of your business.

11.4 Stay updated on industry trends

Ecommerce is an ever-evolving industry, so it's important to stay updated on the latest trends and best practices. I want to emphasize the importance of reading, attending industry conferences and seminars, and joining online communities of Ecommerce professionals. Keep a keen eye on new technologies, emerging strategies, and successful experiences of other industry professionals to constantly adapt and improve your business.

11.5 Be innovative and flexible

Innovation and flexibility are key elements for long-term Ecommerce success. Seek to experiment, explore new opportunities, and quickly adapt to market changes and customer needs. Be open to adopting new technologies, exploring new sales channels, and implementing creative ideas to differentiate yourself from the competition.

In this chapter, we have explored the best practices for long-term Ecommerce success. We have addressed the importance of customer experience, monitoring key metrics, maintaining brand image consistency, staying updated on industry trends, and being innovative and flexible.

We conclude this chapter, hoping that these best practices provide you with a solid foundation for the success of your Ecommerce. Always remember to adapt, improve, and innovate continuously to keep up with an ever-evolving market.

Chapter 12: Explosive Conversions: How to Optimize Your Ecommerce Business to Maximize Sales – "Conversion Checklist"

Before presenting you with the Ecommerce Conversion Checklist, a comprehensive guide that includes over 300 optimization points for your Ecommerce website, I would like to provide a brief introduction. This checklist, once verified, completed, and implemented, will help you maximize conversions and skyrocket your online sales.

Yes, you understood correctly. The Ecommerce Conversion Checklist has been carefully and attentively created to cover all the key aspects necessary to optimize your site and provide an exceptional experience to your visitors. Each point has been selected and organized to provide you with a comprehensive and practical guide, allowing you to focus on critical aspects to improve your Ecommerce's performance.

The checklist encompasses a wide range of categories and will guide you through the fundamental points of user experience, SEO optimization, quality content, personalized offerings, customer reviews, social media marketing, online advertising, email marketing, and much more. With over 300 optimization points, you'll have an exhaustive checklist that will enable you to optimize every aspect of your Ecommerce website.

Each point of the Ecommerce Conversion Checklist has been carefully tested to provide you with the necessary details and instructions to implement the optimizations. You'll find clear explanations, practical tips, and best practices that will help you make the most of every improvement opportunity.

By implementing the Ecommerce Conversion Checklist, you will be able to:

Optimize the user experience to ensure smooth and intuitive navigation on your site, allowing visitors to easily find what they are looking for and complete the purchasing process quickly and effortlessly.

Improve the visibility of your Ecommerce website in search engines by leveraging SEO best practices to increase organic traffic and attract qualified visitors.

Create quality content that informs, engages, and convinces visitors to take the desired action, providing clear information, captivating images, and detailed product descriptions.

Personalize offerings for your customers, using data and insights to deliver targeted and relevant offers that meet their specific needs.

Leverage customer reviews and social proof to build trust and encourage visitors to make purchases on your site.

Strategically use social media marketing, online advertising, and email marketing to effectively reach your target audience and promote your products with targeted messaging.

The Ecommerce Conversion Checklist will guide you step-by-step through each optimization point, allowing you to follow a clear and structured path to improve your Ecommerce's performance right from the start.

We are confident that by implementing the Ecommerce Conversion Checklist, you will be able to double or even triple your conversions and explode your sales. Leave nothing to chance, follow the checklist, and enjoy the tangible results you will achieve.

Get ready to transform your Ecommerce into a powerful and successful sales engine. We can't wait to see your incredible results!

Conversion Checklist

The Ecommerce Conversion Checklist has been structured taking into account the different pages of your site that make up the Ecommerce Funnel. With a total of 304 actions to be taken to optimize the entire website. Here's an overview of the actions to be done for each page:

General Site: 45 actions to be taken

- This includes actions related to site architecture, page organization, navigation, and other general optimizations that apply to the entire Ecommerce site.

Home Page: 21 actions to be taken

- This includes specific optimizations for your main page, such as improving layout, using captivating images and texts, adding strategic call-to-action buttons, and more.

Category Page: 29 actions to be taken

- This includes specific actions for category pages, such as organizing products, implementing search filters, showing sorting options, and improving navigation within categories.

Product Page: 69 actions to be taken

- This is a critical point as it concerns product pages. Actions include optimizing product descriptions, images, customer reviews, providing detailed information, implementing call-to-action buttons, and more.

Cart Page: 25 actions to be taken

- This includes specific actions for the cart page, such as simplifying the checkout process, clearly displaying order summaries, providing clear shipping and payment options, and reassuring customers about transaction security.

Checkout Page: 38 actions to be taken

- This is a crucial point for maximizing conversions. Actions include streamlining the checkout process, reducing required fields, implementing account registration options, providing reliable payment options, and offering assistance during the checkout process.

Thank You Page: 8 actions to be taken

- This includes optimizations for the post-purchase thank you page, such as offering additional offers, inviting customers to leave a review or share their purchase on social media, and providing information on how to contact customer service if needed.

General Landing Page: 69 actions to be taken

- This concerns landing pages used for specific promotions, marketing campaigns, or special offers. Actions include optimizing text and images, implementing contact or registration forms, adding customer testimonials, and ensuring a clear call-to-action.

Optin Page: 10 actions to be taken

- This concerns optin pages used for lead generation, capturing the contact information of potential customers in order to educate them and follow up with our marketing materials, send specific promotions or special offers. Actions include optimizing text and images, implementing contact or registration forms, adding customer testimonials, and ensuring a clear call-to-action.

Total: 314 actions to be taken

- This Ecommerce Conversion Checklist has been designed to be comprehensive and cover every critical aspect of your website. By carefully following the indicated actions, you will be able to optimize each page and significantly improve your Ecommerce's conversions.

So let's get started and dive into the most comprehensive and effective checklist in the world. Resolve all the points listed in the checklist and triple your Ecommerce's Conversion Rate.

Start from the beginning without rushing, analyze each point of your store, verifying and implementing all the suggested changes.

We will now begin exploring the powerful Ecommerce Conversion Checklist, a comprehensive guide that will take you through all the critical points of optimizing your site to maximize conversions and sales, starting with the general points that make up your Ecommerce.

The Conversion Checklist has been divided into different sections to provide you with a complete and detailed view of every key aspect of your Ecommerce. We will start with the first part of the checklist, which focuses on the general critical points of Ecommerce. This section will provide you with a solid foundation for optimization that you can apply to your entire site.

Next, we will delve into the specifics of each level of the Ecommerce funnel, examining and optimizing the key pages that influence the conversion process. From your Home Page to category pages, product pages, cart, and checkout, each stage will be analyzed, and you will be guided through a series of specific actions to maximize conversions at every step.

Finally, we will focus on the thank you page, which is often overlooked but offers a valuable opportunity to further engage customers and encourage them to return to your Ecommerce for future purchases.

Whether you are starting a new Ecommerce or looking to improve an existing one, this Conversion Checklist will provide you with the necessary guidance for success. We are excited to share with you all the critical optimization points and see you achieve extraordinary results in your online business.

Without further ado, let's begin with the first part of the Conversion Checklist, exploring the general critical points of Ecommerce and preparing for a comprehensive optimization at every level of the Ecommerce funnel.

Conversion Checklist "General Site"

- The main pages (home page, landing page, product page) load quickly (no more than 5 seconds) - check speed with Google Page Speed or similar tools.
- Each page has at least one call-to-action (CTA) (even error 404 pages, pages with zero results, error and blog posts, about us page, etc. should have a CTA).
- Clickable elements (such as buttons or links) are clearly visible and prominent (hover function works, rounded corners with subtle gradients, link colors are easily noticeable and underlined).
- The cookie notification bar can be easily closed and approved (within 2 seconds, especially on mobile).
- The site offers a wishlist, which is usually the simplest step to lead visitors to the checkout process and complete the order.

- Button labels and link labels start with a verb and specify a specific action (e.g., "Buy now," "Complete order").
- Non-clickable or non-selectable elements should not have characteristics that suggest they are clickable (no misleading clickable elements where they are not needed).
- There is sufficient spacing between action goals (buttons, forms, contact forms, images, and copy) to prevent users from getting confused and achieving multiple or incorrect goals simultaneously.
- The store offers up-sell and cross-sell opportunities between the product page, checkout page, and thank you page; if the user decides to add another product to the order, they should not be required to re-enter all payment information but should be able to purchase additional products with a simple click.
- The store logo is positioned consistently on every page; clicking the logo takes the user to the most logical page (e.g., home page).

- The website uses subtle micro-animations (e.g., pulses) to emphasize the main CTA on each page.
- The site includes annoying pop-ups at the wrong time (too early in the purchasing process or appearing too late).
- The home page promotes site-wide offers at the top of the page (e.g., Free shipping) with urgency and scarcity triggers ("Today only") and a CTA linked to the desired product ("Buy best-sellers now").
- The top bar contains a prominent site-wide offer with a clear CTA.

Conversion Checklist "Navigation"

- The navigation system is wide and shallow (contains many items per menu level) rather than deep (many menu levels) and should have at least three levels of depth.
- A visible indication is provided for navigation (e.g., showing the active state of the current page).
- Category labels accurately describe category information and what it contains.
- Navigation elements are organized in the most logical order for customers to

understand (less important business information at the bottom and key information prominently displayed, especially on mobile).

- The main navigation includes unnecessary links (e.g., privacy policy, return policy, terms and conditions), which should be placed in the footer, not the main menu.
- The store uses persistent and simple navigation, so categories, the home page, search, and the cart widget are easily accessible at all times, from every page and on every device.

Conversion Checklist "Search Bar"

- The home page prominently features a search box at the top (or top right) of the website.
- The search bar has autocomplete and auto-suggestion options.
- It automatically suggests searches for categories and products.
- The search results page displays the user's searched terms; it is easy to modify and resubmit the search.

- Search results are clear, helpful, and sorted by relevance and the number of retrieved results.
- If no results are found, the search engine ("oops") provides ideas or options to improve the query based on identifiable issues with user input.
- Common queries (as reflected in the analytics) produce useful results and confirmed sales.
- The search engine includes patterns, examples, or tips on how it can be used effectively: verb + object (e.g., search for "men's hat," "blue leggings," "XL pullover").
- The search box is long enough to handle common query lengths and even longer phrases.
- The search box provides results when "Enter" is pressed.
- The search box contains a clearly recognizable magnifying glass icon representing the search function.
- After clicking on the search field and before typing anything, the search

provides suggestions based on recent searches or trending searches.

- The search engine provides automatic spell-check and searches for plurals and synonyms.

Conversion Checklist "Header Cart Widget"

- The cart widget is easily accessible on every page in the top right or bottom corner.
- The mini cart widget includes the total price, total discount, number of items, all items in the cart (on hover), and is visible on every page of the site.
- If the store has a free shipping option, the cart widget clearly indicates how far the user is from qualifying for free shipping.
- Both a cart and checkout link are clearly visible on the mini cart widget.
- The empty cart widget has (on hover) a CTA for "Buy our best-sellers."

Conversion Checklist "Footer"

- The footer highlights the benefits of shopping at the store (e.g., free shipping, returns, refunds, 19,000 products shipped this month, contact information, newsletters).

- The footer contains a "Back to top" link so that users can easily return to the top by clicking a link.
- It is clear that there is a real organization behind the site (e.g., a physical address or a photo of the office or actual people actively working).
- The return policy, privacy policy, and terms and conditions are easily visible on a specific page with a single click.
- The footer displays trust icons/seals (e.g., verified by Norton, warranties, credit cards) along with reassuring copy (e.g., "Shop with confidence").
- The footer includes links to social networks and a total count of likes/followers (to verify credibility).
- The footer includes links to major categories and best-selling products.

Congratulations! You have successfully completed the first part of the Conversion Checklist for Ecommerce, which focused on the critical points of Ecommerce in general. You have gained a solid foundation of knowledge and actions that will help you optimize your website and maximize conversions.

Now it's time to dive into the second part of the checklist, which focuses on your Home Page. The Home Page is often the first impression that visitors have of your Ecommerce site, so it's crucial to make it captivating, intuitive, and engaging. In this section, we will examine specific details and actions to take to ensure that your Home Page is optimized to convert visitors into customers.

You will be guided through best practices for layout, the use of appealing images, strategic content placement, creating persuasive call-to-actions, and much more. By implementing the recommended actions for the Home Page, you will be able to grab visitors' attention from the very beginning and guide them towards desired conversions.

We are excited to accompany you in this crucial phase of optimizing your Ecommerce site. Once you have completed the Home Page section, you will have a clear understanding of how to improve visitor experience and increase conversions. You will be ready to move on to the next part of the Conversion Checklist and tackle categories, products, the cart, checkout, and more.

Continue to follow our guidance, implement the recommended actions, and fully leverage the potential of your Ecommerce site. We are confident that with careful and diligent implementation of the Conversion Checklist, you will see significant improvements in conversions and sales for your business.

We look forward to accompanying you in the next part of the Conversion Checklist for Ecommerce and sharing additional tips and strategies to maximize your site's performance. Together, we will achieve unprecedented levels of success in the world of Ecommerce.

Get ready to face new challenges and transform your Ecommerce into a successful sales machine. We are confident that with our help and your determination, you will achieve extraordinary results in your online business. Let's get started!

Conversion Checklist "Home Page"

- The home page promotes site-wide offers at the top of the page, prominently visible on mobile devices (e.g., Free Shipping, Product Bundles) with urgency and scarcity triggers.

- The home page is professionally designed, not overloaded with unnecessary elements, and creates a positive first impression for visitors.
- Upon landing on the home page, it is immediately clear what the main products the store is selling.
- The home page follows a clear and straightforward visual hierarchy.
- The unique selling proposition (USP or UVP) is clearly stated on the home page (e.g., with a slogan or strong positioning message).
- The home page contains meaningful high-quality graphics, not clip art or stock model images downloaded from Google.
- The home page features one or two visually prominent CTAs above the fold, with relevant copy (e.g., Start Shopping).
- The home page highlights any specific offers, special deals, or time-limited offers at the top.

- The home page showcases the key advantages of shopping at your store (e.g., 'Vegan friendly', 'We donate money to charity', 'Not tested on animals', '19,222 products successfully shipped and delivered this month', 'Money-Back Guarantee').
- The most important product categories are displayed first, with descriptive photos at the top of the home page.
- The store utilizes special category pages (best-sellers, new arrivals, sales, '30% discount', etc.) that guide users into a simple and enticing buying mode.
- There is a shortlist of key products integrated with links on the home page or in the menu.
- The home page provides an option for customers to contact the store (e.g., live chat, email, or phone number).
- The home page displays recently viewed items for returning visitors.
- The founders' story behind the product and the store is showcased, along with their mission and vision (perhaps with a video in the background).

Conversion Checklist "Home Page Social Proof":

- The home page includes general customer reviews or product-specific reviews with a link to the respective product ready to be purchased.
- The home page displays overall store ratings from reputable review sites (e.g., Trustpilot, Trustshop, etc.).
- The home page showcases awards, trust badges, and certificates earned by the store.
- The home page highlights logos of news/blog/celebrity sites where the product/brand has received PR exposure (e.g., 'Used by Fortune 500 executives').
- The home page highlights logos of well-known brands.
- The home page features user-generated photos (e.g., from Instagram).

Congratulations on completing the Home Page section of the Conversion Checklist for Ecommerce! You have taken a significant step towards fully optimizing your website. Now, it's time to move on to the next part of the checklist: Categories.

Category pages are crucial in guiding visitors to their desired products and facilitating their shopping experience. In this section, we will explore key aspects of optimizing category pages to maximize conversions. You will learn how to organize products into logical categories, implement search filters for easy navigation, improve the presentation of sorting options, and much more. The goal is to provide visitors with an effective and satisfying search experience, allowing them to quickly find what they are looking for.

Continuing with the Conversion Checklist, you will be guided through a series of specific actions to optimize category pages and ensure smooth navigation. By implementing the recommended strategies, you can increase the relevance of search results, enhance the display of products, and encourage visitors to further explore your site.

We are excited to accompany you in this part of the Conversion Checklist for Ecommerce and help you achieve outstanding results with your category pages. Prepare to apply best practices, optimize your products, and create intuitive navigation that entices visitors to convert into purchases.

Don't hesitate to fully leverage the Conversion Checklist for Ecommerce, as each recommended action represents an opportunity to improve the performance of your site and increase sales. Continue to follow the guidelines and implement the recommended actions, and you will be on the right path to achieving remarkable results in your online business.

Now, proceed to the Categories section of the Conversion Checklist for Ecommerce and discover how to make category pages a strong asset for your site. We are confident that with your dedication and the application of the provided tips, you will achieve great success in your journey towards ecommerce success.

Conversion Checklist "Category Page General"

- Users can sort the category results page (e.g., by price, "best-selling," "new items," "popular," or "discounted").

- The sorting function is displayed in the top-right corner above the product list/grid.
- The category page has clear and understandable subcategory names.
- The category page utilizes relevant category page design (grid view when images are the main deciding factor and list view when product attributes are the main deciding factor).
- It displays the exact number of products available on each page (whether the page is filtered or not).
- A page description section (approximately 400 words) is placed at the top (visually hidden 90% with "Read more") or at the bottom for SEO purposes.
- It maintains the same vertical position if you navigate to the product page and then back to the category page.

Conversion Checklist "Category Page Product Card/List"

- Relevant products (3-4) are displayed first per row.

- Trending, top-rated, and best-selling items are shown at the top of each category by default.
- Additional product images are shown on hover.
- Consistent image styling is used for better scannability (image type, image background, white space around products, product dimensions, photo angles).
- Consistent product card sizes are used for better scannability.
- The category page clearly indicates which product variants (size, color) are available for each specific product.
- All important information is displayed for each product (highlighted product title, old price, new price, discount, review count, overall star rating, short description, product variants [size, color], short descriptions, product attributes).
- The CTA button is displayed to motivate users to view the product page (ideally on hover).
- Product scarcity is shown with limited availability ("Only 1 left").

- Sold-out items are displayed (e.g., "You just missed it"), so the above scarcity is more convincing.
- Badges are shown on product image thumbnails (e.g., "Fast delivery," "Best-seller," "New," "Top choice," "Trending").
- Customers can provide their email address if the product is currently unavailable; they will be notified when it becomes available.

Conversion Checklist "Category Page Filters"

- The category page offers useful filters (especially on mobile devices) that are easy to understand (applicable only for stores with a large number of products).
- The filters are sufficiently prominent (relevant only for stores where users are inclined to use filters).
- The most popular filters are displayed at the top of the filters.
- Only relevant filters are shown for each category (e.g., screen size for the "Monitor" category).
- It is clearly visible (especially on mobile) that filters are applied, how many there are, and they can be easily removed.

- Users can select multiple filters simultaneously.
- Filters are displayed in a standard position on the left or at the top (below the category name).
- When a filter is selected, the category page updates automatically in real-time (ajax).
- Product filters are sticky and easily accessible at any time.
- Appropriate selectors are used for different types of filters (e.g., color swatches instead of "blue," price range slider where users can enter the minimum and maximum price instead of a predefined list of price ranges).

Congratulations on completing the section on Product Cards in the Conversion Checklist for Ecommerce! You have taken significant steps towards optimizing your website and improving the shopping experience for your visitors. Now, we are preparing to tackle the most important and influential part of all: Product Pages.

Product Pages are the heart of your Ecommerce site. They showcase your products to the public and play a crucial role in convincing visitors to make purchases. In this section, we will explore in detail how to optimize Product Pages to maximize conversions and grow your sales.

We will guide you through a series of specific actions to create engaging product descriptions, use captivating images, provide detailed information, implement customer reviews and testimonials, and much more. Every detail of the Product Pages has a significant impact on visitors' purchasing decisions, and it is essential to fully leverage every opportunity to persuade visitors to convert.

I strongly encourage you to pay close attention to this section and implement the recommended actions carefully. Well-optimized Product Pages are a powerful tool for influencing visitors' purchasing decisions and turning them into satisfied customers. Make sure to provide accurate and engaging descriptions, high-quality images, detailed information, and reviews that instill trust in your brand and products.

Remember that every action you take to optimize the Product Pages can make a difference in converting visitors into paying customers. Take the time to follow the guidelines of the

Conversion Checklist for Ecommerce and implement the recommended actions carefully.

I challenge you not to underestimate the importance of Product Pages and to pay attention to every detail. Remember that every visible, textual, and graphic element can influence visitors' perception of your product. Maximize the potential of this section, and you will see the results reflected in your conversions and sales.

Get ready to tackle this crucial part of the Conversion Checklist for Ecommerce. Implement the recommended actions and fully harness the potential of your Product Pages to grow your online business. We are confident that your attention and dedication will lead to extraordinary results on your path to Ecommerce success.

Conversion Checklist "Product Page General"

- The product page has permanent navigation with the product name prominently displayed, main and secondary product images, collapsible sections with various information and descriptions, availability indicated with scarcity, old price, new price, discount badge, and a CTA that hides when the user scrolls down but reappears when the user scrolls up.

- The product page offers an option for potential customers to ask questions (e.g., live chat, phone number).
- The product page contains breadcrumbs (not applicable to single product stores and direct response landing pages).
- A customer can provide their email address if the product is currently unavailable and be notified when it becomes available.
- Clicking the Back button always takes the user back to the page they came from.

Conversion Checklist "Product Overview (above the CTA area)"

- Product titles are self-descriptive.
- The main product title is visually prominent compared to other content (H1 or H2).
- The product title is less than 65 characters, so it appears fully in Google search results.

- Product subtitles highlight key product benefits and contain powerful words such as easy, incredible, absolute, unique, secret, now, new, exclusive, how, why.
- Product rating summaries are displayed next to the product titles and are linked (with click and scroll) to product reviews (e.g., 4.6, Read 5 reviews).
- A brief list of other key product benefits is placed near the main title and linked to a detailed description (with control arrows).

Conversion Checklist "Product Page Images"

- The main product photo is attractive (let customers decide).
- The main product photo allows easy zooming (especially on mobile devices).
- There is a gallery with several contextual secondary product photos.
- The product gallery displays thumbnails of other available images.
- The product gallery contains videos that showcase the product from various angles.
- The product gallery includes arrows for navigating between images.

- The product gallery supports horizontal scrolling actions on mobile devices or locks in place.
- Images are available for different product variants/sizes.

Conversion Checklist "Product Page CTA"

- The main CTA is the most visible and eye-catching element on the product page and includes the 'add to cart' icon.
- Product variants are easily accessible on mobile devices and large enough with sufficient white space to avoid accidental clicks.
- Selecting product variants is linked to the product gallery and displays images of the chosen product variants.
- A visible reminder is included to select size/color if a customer forgets and clicks 'add to cart' too soon.
- Interactive selectors are used for product variants.
- Gallery image and price are updated in real-time without triggering page reload if necessary.

- Next to size selections (for products with different sizes), a size chart is available (or a link that opens a small popup and easily closes on a mobile device).
- Localized units for products are displayed with different dimensions/measures (e.g., cm, inches, kg).
- Product descriptions mention the model's size and the size of the T-shirt the model is wearing (in the case of clothing).
- Interactive selectors are used for quantity selection instead of dropdown menus (price and quantity are updated in real-time without page reload).
- The CTA clearly explains what will happen when clicked (e.g., Proceed to secure checkout).
- Clear feedback is provided once the product is added to the cart (e.g., a number in the mini-cart widget increases).
- The main CTA indicates once users add a product to the cart (e.g., '[checkmark] Product added to cart' and after 2 seconds '[right arrow] Go to cart').
- The product price is visually significant, especially if discounted.

- The product price is positioned near the main CTA.
- The product price is localized.
- The background color of the main product page differs from other elements to highlight the CTA (e.g., slightly gray).
- Any additional costs or useful information that may apply are displayed near the primary call to action (e.g., additional shipping costs due to product size, VAT).
- If free shipping is offered, it is highlighted near the primary call to action.
- All shipping information is displayed near the main CTA (buyer's location delivery, buyer's country flag, cost, time).
- Product availability is indicated near the main CTA (e.g., 'In stock').
- The old price (with a strike-through) is shown with the new price, and the amount buyers will save (% or $) when the product is on sale.
- Clear information is provided on returns, refunds, and money-back guarantee just below the CTA.
- Commonly used express payment options are displayed and available (e.g., PayPal,

Amazon, Google Pay, Apple Pay, Cash on Delivery, Bank Transfer, Installments, Cryptocurrency). Also useful for direct response landing pages.

- There is an option for installment payments (e.g., Klarna, AfterPay; only for expensive products). Useful for direct response landing pages that do not encourage the user to add more products to the cart.

Conversion Checklist "Product Page Social Proof"

- The product page highlights logos of news/blog/celebrity sites where the product/brand has received public relations exposure (e.g., "Used by Fortune 500 executives").
- Customer reviews are displayed with the review title, customer's product photos, star rating, reviewer's photo, name, last name, 'verified' buyer, occupation, and age.
- Customer reviews visually stand out from other content (ideally on a slightly yellow background).

- The product page contains photos (with faces) of customers using the product happily.
- Overall product star ratings are displayed and can be filtered by star rating.
- The product page displays the number of customers this week/month/ever (e.g., "17,552 products shipped and successfully delivered this month only").
- The product page contains video testimonials.
- The product page displays the number of followers on Facebook, Instagram, TikTok, and Twitter.

Conversion Checklist "Product Page Conversion and AOV Boosters"

- Clear quantity discounts are offered near the main CTA (1x $24.99/piece, [badge 'Top Choice']; 2x €19.99/piece, [badge 'Recommended']; 3x $17.49/piece, ['Best Value' badge]).
- Relevant cross-sell/up-sell products are offered.
- Relevant bundle products are offered with significant discounts.

- Urgency triggers are used (e.g., 'Today Only,' 'Black Friday Offer,' 'Free Bonus,' 'If the order is placed within the next 12 minutes, it will be shipped today') near the main CTA.
- Scarcity triggers are used (e.g., 'Only 3 products left') near the main CTA.
- Customers are shown how many people have viewed and purchased the product in the last 24 hours.
- A store is donating a small percentage of profit to charity and highlights this information.
- The product page contains a "Customers who viewed this product also viewed..." section where users are shown complementary and/or alternative products.

Conversion Checklist "Product Page Description"

- The product description is easy to read (font size, contrast, single column, 75 characters per line, line height of 1.5, maximum length of 4 lines).

- The structure of product information is easy to scan (grouped information, bullet points, highlighted key benefits).
- Page sections ('General,' 'Technical Information') are accordion-style grouped (if longer) and mobile scannable.
- Section titles explain the product's benefits (and subsequently its features).
- Customers are shown everything included in the product (ideally with an accompanying photo, including the shipping box).
- The product page contains frequently asked questions from customers (for each specific product and store-level questions).
- The technical specifications table is legible (different line colors, hover state, not too distant).
- The product page offers comparisons between similar products.
- The product description explains how to use the product in 3 simple steps.
- The product page contains embedded reviews (or screenshots) from social networks (e.g., Facebook posts,

Messenger, WhatsApp, Tweets, Instagram posts, Instagram DMs, Viber, SMS).

Excellent! Now, in addition to the previous sections we have explored, we offer you an incredible BONUS: the Conversion Checklist for Landing Pages. This is a special chapter that will provide you with a detailed guide on how to optimize your Landing Pages to increase conversions and maximize the impact of your marketing campaigns.

Landing Pages are a key element in your digital marketing strategy. They serve as the gateway for visitors coming from ads, email marketing campaigns, or other sources of traffic. A well-optimized Landing Page can make the difference between a visitor abandoning the site and one who converts into a paying customer.

In this special section, we will guide you through a series of specific actions to create persuasive, engaging, and highly converting Landing Pages. You will learn how to structure content in a compelling way, use visually captivating elements, implement persuasive call-to-actions, and much more.

The Conversion Checklist for Landing Pages will provide you with a comprehensive list of points to check and actions to take to optimize your Landing Pages to their fullest potential. By carefully implementing these actions, you will be able to create highly effective Landing Pages that turn visitors into paying customers.

This incredible BONUS is a unique opportunity to significantly improve the performance of your Landing Pages and increase the ROI of your marketing campaigns. Don't miss out on this chance to acquire advanced skills in creating high-performing Landing Pages.

Get ready to dive into the Conversion Checklist for Landing Pages and fully leverage the potential of this incredible BONUS. Follow the step-by-step instructions, implement the recommended actions, and enjoy the tangible results you will achieve.

We are excited to share this special section with you and see you achieve extraordinary results with your Landing Pages. Don't miss the opportunity to further optimize your ecommerce and make a difference in your marketing strategy.

Prepare to transform your Landing Pages into powerful conversion tools and achieve amazing results in your online business.

Conversion Checklist "Landing Page General"

- The Buy button takes the user directly to checkout (or upsell) and bypasses the cart page.
- Permanent navigation with product name, product image, product page sections, availability, old price, new price, discount, and CTA that hides when the user scrolls down but reappears when the user scrolls up.
- The landing page doesn't contain any outbound links (e.g., clickable logo, navigation, and footer).
- The landing page has an option for potential customers to ask questions (e.g., live chat, phone number).

Conversion Checklist "Landing Page Product Overview (Above CTA)"

- Product titles are descriptive.

- The main product title is visually prominent compared to other content.
- The product title is less than 65 characters, so it appears fully in Google search results.
- Subtitles highlight key product benefits and use powerful words like easy, incredible, absolute, unique, secret, now, new, exclusive, how, why.
- Product review summaries are displayed alongside linked product titles (with scroll animation) to product reviews (e.g., 4.6, Read 5 reviews).
- A brief list of key product benefits is placed near the main title and linked to a detailed description (with green control arrows).

Conversion Checklist "Landing Page Images"

- The page layout is standardized (e.g., photo gallery on the left, description and CTA on the right).
- The main product photo is attractive.
- The main product photo allows easy zooming (especially on mobile devices).
- There is a gallery with multiple product photos.

- The product gallery displays thumbnails of other available images.
- The product gallery contains videos showcasing the product.
- The product gallery has arrows for navigating between images.
- The product gallery supports swipe actions on mobile devices.
- Images are available for different product variations/sizes.

Conversion Checklist "Landing Page CTA Area"

- The main CTA is the most visible element on the product page and contains the 'cart' icon.
- Product variations are easily accessible on mobile devices and large enough with sufficient white space to avoid accidental clicks.
- The selection of product variations is linked to the product gallery and displays images of the chosen product variations.
- A visible reminder to select size/color is included if a customer forgets and clicks 'add to cart' too soon.

- Interactive selectors are used for product variations (gallery image and price are updated in real-time without page reloading).
- A size chart is present alongside size selections (for products with different sizes), either as a table or as a link that opens a small popup and easily closes on mobile devices.
- Localized units for products are shown with different dimensions/measures (e.g., cm, inches, kg).
- Product descriptions mention the model's size and the size of the T-shirt the model is wearing (only for clothing).
- Interactive selectors are used for quantity selection instead of dropdown menus (price and quantity are updated in real-time without page reloading).
- The CTA copy clearly explains what will happen when clicked (e.g., Proceed to Secure Checkout).
- The product price is visually important, especially if discounted.
- The product price is positioned near the main CTA.

- The product price is localized.
- The background color of the main CTA differs from other elements (e.g., slightly gray).
- All additional costs that may apply are displayed near the main CTA (e.g., additional shipping costs due to product size, VAT).
- If free shipping is offered, it is highlighted near the main CTA.
- All shipping information is displayed near the main CTA (delivery to the buyer's location, buyer's country flag, cost, time).
- Product availability is indicated near the main CTA (e.g., 'In stock').
- The old price (with a strikethrough) is shown with the new price and the amount buyers will save (% or $) when the product is on sale.
- Clear information is displayed about returns, refunds, and money-back guarantee.
- Commonly used express payment options are displayed and available (e.g., PayPal, Amazon, Google Pay, Apple Pay). Useful for direct response landing pages.

- An option for installment payments is available (e.g., Klarna, AfterPay; only for expensive products). Useful for direct response landing pages that do not encourage adding more products to the cart.
- The landing page highlights the main advantages of shopping with you (e.g., 'Vegan-friendly', 'We donate to charity', 'Not tested on animals', '19,222 products shipped and successfully delivered this month').

Conversion Checklist "Landing Page Social Proof"

- The product page highlights logos of news/blog/celebrity sites where the product/brand has received media exposure (e.g., 'Used by Fortune 500 executives').
- Customer reviews are displayed with review titles, customer product photos, star ratings, reviewer photo, name and surname, 'verified' buyer, occupation, and age.

- Customer reviews visually stand out from other content (ideally on a slightly yellow background).
- The product page contains customer photos (with faces) showing how customers (happy) use the product.
- Overall star ratings for the product are displayed and can be filtered based on star ratings.
- The product page displays the number of customers this week/month/ever (e.g., '19,222 products shipped and successfully delivered this month').
- The product page contains video testimonials.
- The product page displays the number of followers on Facebook and Twitter.

Landing Page Conversion and AOV Boosters

- After clicking the 'Buy' button, the user is taken to an upsell variant where a cheaper second item (of the same or complementary product) is offered.
- Clear quantity discounts are offered near the main CTA (1x $24.99/piece, [Top Choice badge]; 2x $19.99/piece,

[Recommended badge]; 3x $17.49/piece, [Best Value badge]).

- Relevant cross-sell/up-sell products are offered.
- Relevant bundle products are offered with significant discounts.
- Urgency triggers are used (e.g., 'Today only', 'Black Friday Offer', 'Free Bonus', 'If the order is placed within the next 12 minutes, it will be shipped today') near the main CTA.
- Scarcity triggers are used (e.g., 'Only 3 products left') near the main CTA.
- Customers are shown how many people have viewed and purchased the product in the last 24 hours.
- A store is donating a small percentage of profits to charity and highlights this information.
- The product page contains 'Visitors who viewed this product also viewed...' where users are shown complementary or alternative products.

Conversion Checklist "Landing Page Product Description"

- The product description is easy to read (font size, contrast, single column, 75 characters per line, line height 1.5, max length of 4 lines).
- The structure of product information is easy to scan (grouped information, bullet points, highlighted key benefits).
- Page sections ('General', 'Technical Information') are accordion-style (if longer) and mobile-friendly.
- Section titles explain the product benefits (rather than features).
- Customers are shown everything included with the product (ideally with an included photo).

Now it's time to explore the Conversion Checklist for the Cart Page, another crucial part of an Ecommerce funnel. The Cart Page is the critical transition point where visitors confirm their purchases and prepare for checkout. Optimizing this page is essential to maximize conversions and ensure that visitors successfully complete the purchase process.

In the Conversion Checklist for the Cart Page, we will guide you through a series of specific actions that will help you create an optimized and engaging Cart Page. These actions will enable you to streamline the checkout process, provide a clear and intuitive order summary, offer flexible shipping and payment options, and more.

The first thing to consider is usability. The Cart Page should be intuitive, with a clear layout and simple navigation. Ensure that visitors can easily add, remove, or modify products in their cart. Minimize distractions and simplify the checkout process to make the shopping experience quick and seamless.

In addition to usability, it's important to provide a comprehensive and accurate order summary. Make sure visitors can easily view the products in their cart, including details such as price, quantity, and variants. Also, include editing options, such as the ability to modify quantity or remove a product directly from the Cart Page.

Offering flexible shipping and payment options is another key aspect of optimizing the Cart Page. Provide a selection of shipping methods based on your customers' preferences and clearly communicate estimated delivery times. As for payments, consider including various options such as credit cards, PayPal, or other popular payment services.

Furthermore, create a sense of security and trust on the Cart Page. Display security certificate logos, provide a customer support number or link to contact information, and consider including testimonials from satisfied customers or refund guarantees to reassure visitors.

By carefully following the Conversion Checklist for the Cart Page, you will be able to optimize this crucial stage in the purchase process. By creating a user-friendly, informative, and engaging Cart Page, you will increase the chances of visitors completing the purchase and becoming satisfied customers.

Do not underestimate the importance of the Cart Page in your Ecommerce. Take the time to follow the recommended actions and fully harness the potential of this page to maximize conversions and grow your sales.

Get ready to tackle the Conversion Checklist for the Cart Page and apply best practices to optimize this fundamental phase of the purchase process. We are confident that with your attention and dedication, you will achieve outstanding results in your online business.

Conversion Checklist "Cart Page General"

- The overall design of the cart is clear and organized.
- Urgency triggers are used ("Your items are reserved for 10 minutes," "Order in the next 12 minutes for same-day shipping").
- The cart page clearly informs the user how far they are from the threshold for free shipping (or a 3% discount).
- If the user has already reached the threshold for free shipping, the cart highlights it (e.g., bold, green).
- When the user returns to the site, the items they added to the cart are still there.
- All important product information is displayed in the cart (title, image, chosen variant, quantity, price).
- The correct product image is shown for the selected product variant (e.g., red dress).
- The cart allows for modifying the quantity of the product and updates automatically.

- The user can easily remove an item from the cart.
- The cart displays the estimated delivery date.
- Scarcity triggers are shown next to each item ("Only 1 item in stock") in a prominent color (e.g., red, orange).
- The cart provides an easy way to contact the store's customer support (e.g., live chat, email, phone number).
- Information about returns, refunds, and a money-back guarantee is displayed (if on external pages, a small pop-up window is shown instead of redirecting the customer away from the cart).
- The cart offers a way to enter a coupon code but with a hidden input field (so users won't search for coupon codes on Google).
- The cart offers upsell/cross-sell products (affordable) with benefits and urgency ("Now or never") and a special discount (e.g., 50% OFF).
- Customers can "save products/cart for later" instead of removing them.

Conversion Checklist "Cart Page CTA Area"

- The subtotal price is prominent and positioned near the main CTA.
- Estimated taxes are displayed.
- The buyer is shown how much they will save on the entire purchase near the main action.
- The main CTA includes what will happen next ("Proceed to secure checkout") and is the most important and duplicated element at the top and bottom of the page.
- The main CTA ("Proceed to secure payment") includes a lock-shaped icon on a distinctive background (gray).
- Below the main call-to-action, there is a trust icon/seal badge (e.g., Norton verified) along with reassuring copy "Buy with confidence."
- Alternative payment options are shown below the main CTA button (e.g., PayPal, Amazon Pay, Google Pay).
- Images of all available payment methods are displayed (e.g., Klarna) with clear information on monthly payment and duration (especially useful for higher-priced products).

- A secondary CTA button "Continue shopping" is available on the cart page.

Let's now proceed with the analysis of the Conversion Checklist for the Checkout Page, one of the most critical parts in an Ecommerce funnel. The Checkout Page is the culmination of the purchasing process, where visitors enter their payment information and confirm the order. Optimizing this page is essential to facilitate the completion of the purchase and maximize conversions.

In the Conversion Checklist for the Checkout Page, we will guide you through a series of specific actions to create an optimized and user-friendly Checkout Page. These actions will help simplify the checkout process, reduce friction, and create a seamless experience for visitors.

The first thing to consider is simplicity. The Checkout Page should be clean, intuitive, and free of distractions. Minimize the number of required fields, allowing visitors to enter payment and shipping information quickly and smoothly. Eliminate any unnecessary elements that could distract visitors and slow down the checkout process.

Furthermore, ensure that the Checkout Page is secure and instills confidence in visitors. Display security certificate logos, provide clear information about transaction security, and use an HTTPS connection to protect customers' personal data. Security is a fundamental element to make visitors feel comfortable during the checkout process.

Implement flexible payment options as well. Offer different payment methods such as credit cards, PayPal, bank transfer, or other popular services. Ensure that the payment options are clear and easy to select, reducing friction and providing alternatives that cater to your customers' preferences.

Another important consideration is cost transparency. Ensure that visitors are clearly informed about any additional costs such as shipping fees, taxes, or fees. Avoid negative surprises during checkout and display a detailed order summary so that customers can review the details before finalizing the purchase.

Lastly, provide support during the checkout process. Provide a customer support number or a live chat system to address visitors' questions or provide immediate assistance. Show your commitment to providing quality service and support customers throughout the entire purchase journey.

By carefully following the Conversion Checklist for the Checkout Page, you can create an optimized Checkout Page that reduces friction and increases conversions. Maximize usability, security, cost transparency, and customer support to provide a seamless checkout experience.

Do not underestimate the importance of the Checkout Page in your Ecommerce business. Take the necessary time to follow the recommended actions and fully leverage the potential of this page to maximize conversions and ensure that visitors become satisfied customers.

Prepare yourself to tackle the Conversion Checklist for the Checkout Page and apply best practices to optimize this crucial phase of the purchasing process. We are confident that with your attention and dedication, you will achieve extraordinary results in your online business.

Conversion Checklist "Checkout Page General"

- The checkout allows the user to make a purchase as a guest (avoid unnecessary registrations).
- The site provides good feedback during checkout (e.g., a progress bar indicating where the user is in the checkout process).
- If there is a multi-step checkout, it is clear what will happen after clicking the CTA.
- The form avoids making the user start over in case of an error.
- Immediately before committing to the purchase, the site shows the user a clear order summary.
- Below the main call to action, there is a trust icon/seal (e.g., verified by Norton) along with reassuring copy "Buy with confidence".
- The checkout does not contain outbound links (e.g., clickable logo, navigation, and footer).
- The site's privacy policy is easy to find, especially on pages that require personal information, and the policy is simple and clear.

- Checkout offers a simple way to get in touch with the store's customer support (e.g., live chat, email, phone number).
- The main call to action is the most important element on the payment page.

Conversion Checklist "Checkout Page Conversion and AOV Boosters"

- After the payment page and before the thank you page, there is an upsell step where the user can add another product to the existing order.
- The payment page includes upsell orders (e.g., "Skip the line," "Express shipping," "Gift wrapping," "Package insurance") with prices below $3.
- Urgency triggers are used ("Your items are reserved for 10 minutes," "If your order is completed in the next 12 minutes, it will be shipped today").

Checkout Page Login and Registration

- Checkout allows users to log in so that they don't have to enter all the information again.

- During registration, the password selection process is not overly complicated with unnecessary requirements.
- Password recovery is easy.

Conversion Checklist "Checkout Page Forms"

- The layout of input fields is as simple as possible (ideally in a single column).
- The payment page has the minimum number of input fields necessary to complete the purchase.
- The input fields on the payment page use "floating labels" so that the user can see both the field name and its content simultaneously.
- The user's email address is requested first so that the store can contact them if they exit the checkout.
- Input fields contain hints (e.g., Email: example@gmail.com) to reduce user cognitive load.
- The payment page has an option to check "billing address is the same as shipping," so the user doesn't need to enter the same address twice.

- Selecting a payment option (e.g., radio buttons) is easily accessible on mobile devices.
- Visual prompts for credit card details are included, such as an image indicating where to find the CVV code.
- Credit card input fields are displayed on a gray background for increased (perceived) reliability.
- Users can easily navigate between input fields within a form using the "Tab" key.
- When entering data in a numeric-only input field (e.g., ZIP code, phone number), a numeric keyboard is displayed on mobile devices.
- When entering an email address, a keyboard with dedicated buttons for "@" and ".com" is displayed on mobile devices.
- The width of the input field indicates the amount and format of the data to be entered (e.g., the ZIP code input is narrower than the address field), including credit card inputs.
- Optional and mandatory fields are easily distinguishable.

- If requesting a phone number, we need to explain next to/below the input that it is only for delivery information.
- Checkout uses a database of street addresses to prevent users from mistyping the address.
- Input fields use inline validation with a prominent green/red border and arrow/x sign (e.g., if the email is entered correctly).
- User doesn't need to enter the same information more than once.
- Checkout utilizes autofill where possible (e.g., when the user types the ZIP code, the city is automatically filled in).
- If the user leaves the checkout and then returns, the input fields will have been saved so they can continue where they left off.
- Input fields have an option (X icon on the right side) to clear the content with a single click.

Let's now move on to the final part of the Conversion Checklist, dedicated to the Thank You Page. The Thank You Page is a crucial moment in the purchasing process as it allows you to express gratitude for the completed transaction and provide additional information or offers to customers. Optimizing this page can help maintain customer interest and encourage future interactions with your brand.

In the Conversion Checklist for the Thank You Page, we will guide you through a series of specific actions to create an effective and engaging Thank You Page. These actions will help you maintain customer attention, encourage further actions, and build a lasting relationship with them.

The first thing to consider is a genuine expression of gratitude. Thank customers for choosing your Ecommerce and completing their purchase. An authentic thank-you message can make customers feel appreciated and strengthen their connection with your brand.

Additionally, consider including additional information or offers. Use the Thank You Page as an opportunity to provide customers with additional order details such as confirmation numbers, a summary of purchased products, and shipping information. You can also offer discounts or future promotions to incentivize customers to return to your Ecommerce and make new purchases.

Incorporate social media sharing options as well. Provide sharing buttons that allow customers to recommend your Ecommerce and the purchased products to their friends and followers. This can amplify your brand's visibility and attract potential new customers.

Furthermore, seize the opportunity to collect feedback from customers. Ask them to provide a review or evaluation of their purchasing experience. This feedback can be valuable for improving your internal processes and sharing positive testimonials with other potential customers.

Finally, consider including cross-selling or upselling elements. Offer related products or upgrade options that may interest customers based on their previous purchases. This can increase the average order value and provide a personalized experience that demonstrates care and attention to customers' needs.

By carefully following the Conversion Checklist for the Thank You Page, you can create an engaging Thank You Page that maintains customer interest and engagement. Use this page as an opportunity to strengthen the relationship with customers, provide additional information, and encourage further actions.

Do not underestimate the importance of the Thank You Page in your Ecommerce. Fully leverage the potential of this page to provide a positive and memorable customer experience, and establish a solid foundation for future interactions.

Prepare yourself to tackle the final part of the Conversion Checklist for the Thank You Page and implement the best practices to optimize this crucial phase of the purchasing process. We are confident that with your attention and dedication, you will achieve extraordinary results in your online business.

Conversion Checklist "Thank You Page General"

- The thank you page clearly indicates that the user has successfully completed the purchase and congratulates them.

- The thank you page clearly summarizes what was in the order.
- The thank you page clearly indicates when the package will arrive and with which courier/delivery service.
- The thank you page provides the user with an easy way to contact the store owner (e.g., live chat, email, phone number).
- The thank you page explains to the user how to track their package.

Conversion Checklist "Thank You Page Conversion and AOV Booster"

- The thank you page offers the user the opportunity to purchase additional items/quantities of the same product at a lower price, or to buy another complementary product, with a clear explanation that these additional items will be combined with the recently placed order.
- The thank you page offers the user a coupon code that they can use for their next purchase or share with their friends.
- The user receives a summary of all information in their confirmation email

(product summary, upsells, coupon code found on the thank you page, etc.).

I'm pleased to introduce you to an exclusive BONUS section of the Conversion Checklist that we are adding to the book: Opt-in Page Optimization.

This section is a unique opportunity to learn best practices and advanced strategies to maximize conversions through the optimization of one of the most important pages in your marketing funnel.

The Opt-in Page is crucial for acquiring email addresses of potential customers interested in your offer and building a list of qualified contacts. By optimizing this page, you will be able to improve the conversion of users visiting your website and increase the number of subscribers to your list.

In the BONUS section of Opt-in Page Optimization, we will provide you with a detailed checklist of specific actions you can take to maximize the effectiveness of your Opt-in Page. Each point on the checklist has been carefully selected to guide you in creating a persuasive, engaging, and highly converting page.

You will learn how to write attention-grabbing headlines that capture visitors' attention and persuasive descriptions that clearly communicate the value of your offer. You will discover how to create effective opt-in forms, compelling call-to-action statements, and how to use engaging visual elements to enhance the impact of your page.

Additionally, we will provide you with tips on how to incorporate testimonials, social proof, and trust elements that increase the credibility of your offer and encourage visitors to provide their information. There will also be suggestions on how to optimize your Opt-in Page for mobile devices, considering the growing number of users accessing the web from smartphones and tablets.

This BONUS section is a valuable addition to your optimization journey. Not only will you improve your ability to capture qualified leads, but also the effectiveness of your marketing and communication strategies.

Don't miss the opportunity to deepen your skills and acquire additional tools to create highly performing Opt-in Pages. Use this section as a practical guide to implement immediate and lasting improvements to your lead acquisition strategy.

Get ready to make the most of this BONUS section of Opt-in Page Optimization and achieve amazing results in your online business. We look forward to seeing you succeed in acquiring new contacts and growing your target audience.

Conversion Checklist "Optin Page":

- Clear Objective: Define the goal of your Opt-in Page, which could be collecting email addresses, getting webinar sign-ups, or any other desired conversion action.
- Catchy Headline: Create a headline that grabs the visitors' attention and entices them to continue. It should be clear, engaging, and communicate the value of your offer.
- Persuasive Description: Write a description that clearly explains the benefits visitors will get from the opt-in and how it will solve their problems or

meet their needs. Use persuasive language to create a sense of urgency or excitement.

- Opt-in Form: Include a well-positioned and user-friendly opt-in form to allow visitors to enter their information. Only request essential information, such as name and email address, to minimize friction.
- Clear Call-to-Action: Use a clear and impactful call-to-action (CTA) to guide visitors to take the desired action. Ensure that the CTA stands out visually and is prominently positioned on the page.
- Captivating Visual Elements: Use relevant images or videos to capture visitors' attention and enhance the visual experience of the page. Ensure that the images are high-quality and aligned with the message and offer of your Opt-in Page.
- Testimonials and Social Proof: Include testimonials or social proof that demonstrate the validity and effectiveness of your offer. Positive customer reviews or success statistics can increase visitors' trust in providing their data.

- Trust and Privacy Elements: Display security logos or seals that indicate the protection of visitors' personal data. Also, provide a link to your privacy policy to reassure visitors that their data will be handled appropriately and securely.
- Mobile-Friendly: Ensure that your Opt-in Page is optimized for mobile devices as more people access the web through smartphones or tablets. Verify that the page is easily navigable and readable on smaller screens.
- Testing and Optimization: Don't forget to regularly test your Opt-in Page and analyze data to identify areas for improvement. Try different versions of headlines, descriptions, CTA colors, and placements to determine which combinations work best for achieving conversions.

Congratulations on exploring and completing all 314 points of the Conversion Checklist! You have done an extraordinary job optimizing your Ecommerce website and maximizing conversions. Now you have a solid foundation of knowledge and specific actions to achieve success in your online business.

It's important to emphasize that completing all the points of the Conversion Checklist requires commitment and dedication. However, every action you have taken is an important step towards achieving your sales and growth goals in the world of Ecommerce.

I strongly encourage you not to underestimate the importance of each individual point in the Conversion Checklist. Even small optimizations can make a big difference in generating more conversions and increasing the success of your online business.

Now, push yourself further and conclude your learning journey with the final chapter of the book. After reading this concluding chapter, you will have the opportunity to put into practice the strategies, tactics, and advanced techniques to exponentially grow your Ecommerce business.

Don't miss the opportunity to deepen your knowledge and acquire additional tools to tackle market challenges and surpass the competition. This book represents added value that will help you consolidate your know-how and develop a winning mindset in Ecommerce.

Prepare yourself to successfully conclude your learning journey. Follow the guidance of the final chapter closely and take advantage of all the tips, strategies, and advice to become number one in your market niche.

Remember, success in Ecommerce is not a one-time achievement but a continuous journey of learning, adapting, and improving. Maintain an attitude open to innovation and change, and you will be able to face future challenges and seize emerging opportunities in the industry.

I wish you the utmost success in your journey in Ecommerce. Continue investing in your professional growth, implement the acquired knowledge, and never stop pursuing excellence in your online business. We are confident that you will achieve extraordinary results and become a true leader in your field.

Conclusion

Congratulations! You have reached the end of our book dedicated to Ecommerce optimization and achieving success in the digital world. Throughout our journey, we have explored numerous key aspects of marketing, online selling, and conversion, providing you with tools, strategies, and a comprehensive checklist to achieve extraordinary results in your business.

We started by examining the importance of Ecommerce and the impact that the rapidly evolving world of technology and artificial intelligence is having on this industry. We emphasized the urgency of adapting to changes and embracing new solutions to remain competitive in an increasingly aggressive market.

Next, we delved into creating an extraordinary shopping experience, focusing on website design, usability, and optimization. We explored the importance of captivating product presentation, smooth checkout process, and engaging web pages to maintain customer interest and maximize conversions.

We then discussed the importance of niche research in the Ecommerce industry and the need to identify and target the ideal audience. We provided tips on how to pinpoint your Unique Selling Proposition (USP) and differentiate yourself from the competition by leveraging your unique strengths.

Our Conversion Checklist has proven to be a powerful weapon in your arsenal of optimization tools. Through over 300 checklists and optimizations divided by pages and key stages, you had the opportunity to analyze and implement best practices to optimize every aspect of your Ecommerce business. From the Home Page to Landing Pages, Categories to Product Pages, Cart to Checkout, and Thank You Page, every detail has been considered to maximize conversions and generate successful sales.

We also explored the power of social media and content marketing, providing you with advice on how to leverage these platforms to engage your audience and amplify your brand visibility.

You also learned about the importance of search engine optimization (SEO) and online advertising (PPC), discovering how to best utilize these strategies to increase qualified traffic to your Ecommerce website.

Lastly, we introduced the significance of having an effective Conversion Funnel in your Ecommerce business. We showed you how to guide visitors through the purchase journey, maximize conversions, and build a lasting relationship with customers.

We are grateful for the time you have dedicated to reading this book and your commitment to learning and implementing the strategies presented. We are confident that with your passion, dedication, and the use of all available resources, you will achieve success in your online business.

We encourage you to put into practice everything you have learned and use the Conversion Checklist as a constant guide for optimizing your Ecommerce business. Remember that optimization is not a final goal but an ongoing process. Stay open to learning, exploring new strategies, and monitoring results to adapt to the changing market needs and continue growing.

Success in Ecommerce requires time, commitment, and dedication. However, if you stay focused, follow best practices, and implement the strategies described in this book, we are confident that you will achieve your business goals and become a leader in your niche.

Thank you again for joining us on this journey of Ecommerce optimization. We wish you the utmost success and the satisfaction of seeing your business grow and thrive. Keep dreaming big, adapting to change, and pursuing your ambitions.

Goodbye and continued success in your extraordinary Ecommerce adventure!

Printed in Great Britain
by Amazon